Best Easy Day Hikes Series

Best Easy Day Hikes
Blue Ridge Parkway

Second Edition

Randy Johnson

FALCONGUIDES

GUILFORD, CONNECTICUT
HELENA, MONTANA

AN IMPRINT OF GLOBE PEQUOT PRESS

FALCONGUIDES®

Copyright © 2003, 2010 by Morris Book Publishing LLC

FalconGuides is an imprint of Globe Pequot Press.

Falcon, FalconGuides, and Outfit Your Mind are registered trademarks of Morris
Book Publishing LLC.

Maps by Daniel Lloyd © Morris Book Publishing LLC

The Library of Congress has cataloged the earlier edition as follows:
Johnson, Randy, 1951–
Best easy day hikes, Blue Ridge Parkway / Randy Johnson.—1st ed.
  p. cm.—(A Falcon guide) (Best easy day hikes series)
  ISBN 978-0-7627-1069-0
  1. Hiking—Blue Ridge Parkway (N.C. and Va.)—Guidebooks. 2. Trails—Blue
Ridge Parkway (N.C. and Va.)—Guidebooks. 3. Blue Ridge Parkway (N.C. and
Va.)—Guidebooks. I. Title. II. Series. III. Series: Best easy day hikes series

GV199.42.B65J62 2003
917.55—dc21

                                2003048317

ISBN 978-0-7627-5526-4

Printed in the United States of America
10 9 8 7 6 5 4 3 2 1

Contents

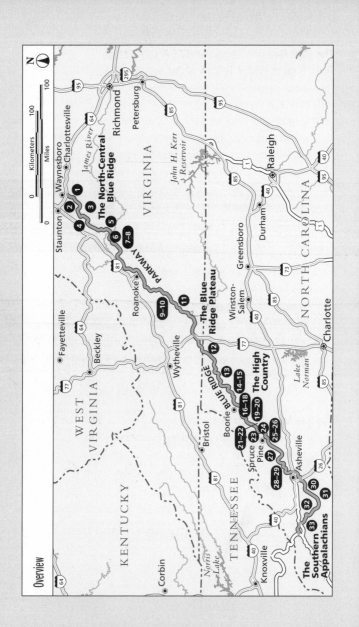

Overview

The High Country: Mileposts 276.4 (US 421 at Deep Gap) to 384.7 (US 74 at Asheville) 77

The Southern Appalachians: Mileposts 384.7 (US 74 at Asheville) to 469.1 (US 441 at Great Smoky Mountains NP) 134

Help Us Keep This Guide Up to Date

Every effort has been made by the author and editors to make this guide as accurate and useful as possible. However, many things can change after a guide is published—trails are rerouted, regulations change, facilities come under new management, etc.

We would appreciate hearing from you concerning your experiences with this guide and how you feel it could be improved and kept up to date. While we may not be able to respond to all comments and suggestions, we'll take them to heart and we'll also make certain to share them with the authors. Please send your comments and suggestions to the following address:

Globe Pequot Press
Reader Response/Editorial Department
P.O. Box 480
Guilford, CT 06437

Or you may e-mail us at:

editorial@GlobePequot.com

Author Randy Johnson is also happy to hear from readers. Please visit his Web site, where you'll find multimedia features about hiking and more information about Randy and his books: www.randyjohnsonbooks.com

Thanks for your input, and happy trails!

Introduction

With the 2010 arrival of the Blue Ridge Parkway's seventy-fifth anniversary, there has never been a better time to explore what travel writers continually call "America's most scenic highway." Stretches of road elsewhere in the United States may indeed be spectacular, but nothing matches this manicured, uniquely uncommercialized half-a-thousand-mile thoroughfare through the lofty heart of America's first frontier. That's what makes the Parkway a globally recognized icon of the American road.

Scenery aside, the recent completion of the Parkway's main visitor center in Asheville and the ongoing finalization of the Blue Ridge Music Center near the Virginia–North Carolina state line are reminders that the experience just keeps getting richer for visitors. A Parkway vacation—truly tackling the length of the roadway from the southern end of Shenandoah National Park in Virginia to Great Smoky Mountains National Park in North Carolina—is a singular experience, a dazzling juncture of earth and sky. Shenandoah's Skyline Drive adds another 100 miles.

Most of the time spent in the Southern mountains—in a car or on foot—involves either going up or coming down. But the Parkway follows almost continually along the crest—truly a skyline traverse.

At the Parkway's 45-mile-per-hour speed limit, the drive could be completed in eleven hours. But the point of this book is that it shouldn't. With vistas beckoning from dozens of overlooks, and trails everywhere, this is a motorized wander that could—and surely should—be given at least a week. The Parkway is a visual feast of vignettes every step or mile of the way.

The Parkway isn't literally a national park, but it is a unit of the National Park Service—and the nation's most visited one at that. More than half the population of the United States lives within a day's drive of the Parkway. Average annual visitation hovers just below 20 million; 2003 set the record at 23.5 million.

Best of all, this national treasure has trails along its entire length, making the Parkway a perfect destination for hikers. Indeed, a drive on this high road is a motorized metaphor for the trail experience itself. The Parkway is an Appalachian Trail for autos. But don't just settle for looking through the windshield—getting out of the car is a must. Nevertheless, the wonder of this motor trail is that what you see while driving is a lot like what you see in the woods. That includes wildlife.

Be on the road early or late and you'll likely have to stop and sit amazed behind the wheel as a herd of deer gambol across the road. Ravens soar with the air currents above evergreen-covered summits. Peregrine falcons, reintroduced at Parkway-adjacent sites since 1984, now nest and dive all along the road. Flocks of wild turkeys, also successfully reintroduced, prefer trailside Parkway meadows.

There's culture as well. Since our nation's earliest westward migrations, the fertile valleys to the east and west of the Blue Ridge Mountains have filled up with farms, towns, and eventually cities. A relative few of those newcomers, among them Scots-Irish and Germans, settled into the very highest elevations of the Blue Ridge and adjacent ranges. Long traditions of music and crafts were thus preserved in these storied hollows. In some ways, Appalachian families were living a pioneering lifestyle long after the West was settled.

Luckily for today's hikers and motorists, early mountain farms and cabins—even a mill—have been preserved at key places along the Parkway, and they impart a sense of what life on the heights must have been like. These exhibits incorporate some of the Parkway's shorter, tamer trails, but they're deeply insightful and worth a wander. Noteworthy stops include the Mountain Farm Trail at Humpback Rocks (Milepost 5.8), Trails Cabin at Smart View Picnic Area (Milepost 154.5), the Johnson Farm at Peaks of Otter (Milepost 85.9), and Mabry Mill (Milepost 176.2).

Handcrafts were essential for survival in this "land of do without." That rich tradition of crafts comes to life in a variety of places on and adjacent to the Parkway. In North Carolina, don't miss the Northwest Trading Post (Milepost 258.6), the Parkway Craft Center in Moses H. Cone Memorial Park (Milepost 294.0), and the Folk Art Center near Asheville (Milepost 382.0).

The Parkway's craft centers and mountain lifestyle exhibits are just the beginning. Skilled crafters often demonstrate their skills at the Parkway's various craft centers. Reenactors at the lifestyle exhibits depict the kinds of domestic and commercial activities it took to wrest a living from a harsh climate and primitive facilities. If you make time for these programs, an amazing part of America's past will come to life for you.

The National Park Service also tries to remind Parkway travelers of the past by leasing lands along the road for farming and other traditional activities. And while you surely will see vacation homes perched in plain sight of the road (Who wouldn't want a perpetual Parkway view?), organizations such as the Blue Ridge Parkway Foundation (336-721-0260; www.brpfoundation.org) and Friends of the Blue Ridge Parkway (704-687–8722 or 800-228-7275; www.blueridgefriends.org) purchase land and scenic easements to preserve the Parkway's viewshed and update visitor centers and other facilities.

And of course the Parkway offers more than a dozen formal picnic areas and dozens of roadside tables at overlooks. There are also nine formal campgrounds. You can reserve sites ahead of time at three of the campgrounds—Julian Price Memorial Park, Linville Falls, and Mount Pisgah—online at www.recreation.gov or toll-free at (877) 444-6777. The Parkway also offers four lodges and a variety of restaurants. More details on these facilities are provided in the introductions to each section of the Parkway.

The Blue Ridge Parkway Web site (www.nps.gov/blri/planyourvisit/brochures.htm) provides extensive up-to-date information about facilities on the Parkway, including PDFs of many trail maps and visitor brochures. Among the publications available online is the park newspaper, *Parkway Milepost,* also found at visitor centers. A separate "Trip Planner" publication is currently available only at visitor centers, and it also includes the Parkway trail maps

Using This Guide

What Is a Best Easy Day Hike?

This hiking guide is an abridged version of *Hiking the Blue Ridge Parkway*. This guide is designed for anyone who uses the Parkway—America's longest and most popular national park—to allow readers to choose hikes best suited to their abilities and time available. Most of the hikes are Parkway "leg-stretchers" that are such an accessible part of a Parkway trip. All the hikes are on well-marked trails that are easy to follow. Most are suitable for novice hikers, families with children, and seniors; and most are accessible right from the Parkway itself.

How This Guide Is Organized

The hikes in this book are organized from north to south, following the Parkway from its northernmost point on Afton Mountain near Waynesboro, Virginia, south to its southern terminus in Cherokee, North Carolina—nearly 470 miles away.

Zero Impact

Visiting a national park such as the Blue Ridge Parkway is like going to a famous art museum. Obviously you do not want to leave your mark on an art treasure in the museum. If every visitor to the museum left one little mark, the piece of art would quickly be destroyed—and of what value is a big building full of abused art? The same goes for a natural area such as the Blue Ridge, which is as magnificent and as valuable as any masterpiece by any artist. If we all left one little mark on the landscape, the Parkway would soon be despoiled.

A wilderness can accommodate plenty of human use as long as everybody behaves. But a few thoughtless or uninformed visitors can ruin it for everybody who follows. The need for good manners applies to all visitors, not just hikers.

Most of us know better than to litter—in or out of the parks and forests. Be sure you leave nothing, regardless of how small it is, along the trail or at your campsite. This means you should pack out everything, including orange peels, cigarette butts, and gum wrappers. Also pick up any trash that others have left behind.

Follow the main trail. Avoid cutting switchbacks and walking on vegetation beside the trail. In the mountains some terrain is very fragile, so stay on the trail if possible. Don't pick up souvenirs, such as rocks, antlers, or wildflowers.

Avoid making loud noises that may disturb others. Remember, sound travels easily along the ridges and through the hollows. Be courteous.

Consider visiting a Parkway restroom before your hike. In the woods, bury human waste 6 to 8 inches deep and pack out used toilet paper. This is a good reason to carry a lightweight trowel (especially for backpackers). Keep waste at least 300 feet away from any water source.

Finally, a point that bears repeating: If you carry something onto the trail, consume it or carry it out.

Three Zero-Impact Principles

- Leave with everything you brought in.
- Leave no sign of your visit.
- Leave the landscape as you found it.

Ranking the Hikes

Easiest

Most Challenging

Map Legend

══════	Blue Ridge Parkway
═══⟨81⟩═══	Interstate Highway
═══⟨501⟩═══	U.S. Highway
═══⟨56⟩═══	State Highway
──────	Local Road
═ ═⟨1238⟩═ ═	Unpaved Road
▬▬▬▬▬	Featured Trail
──────	Trail
─ ─ · ─ · ─	State Line
～～～	River/Creek
⬭	Body of Water
⊛	Capital
⦿	City
‿‿	Bridge
▲	Camping
•—•	Gate
❓	Information Center
🅿	Parking
⌣	Pass
▲	Peak
🏕	Picnic Area
■	Point of Interest/Structure
🚻	Restroom
○	Town
❶	Trailhead
🏞	Viewpoint/Overlook
≋	Waterfall

The North-Central Blue Ridge

*Mileposts 0.0 (I-64 at Shenandoah NP) to
121.4 (US 220 at Roanoke, Virginia)*

The northernmost 120 miles of the Parkway is
the perfect introduction to the Blue Ridge. This
is the Blue Ridge at its most definitive—the
Appalachians, rearing sharply above the Piedmont to the
east and the Shenandoah Valley to the west.

Indeed, the ridge seems sharper here than it does in
Shenandoah National Park, just north of the Parkway. The
100 miles of Shenandoah's Skyline Drive is a nice prelude
that turns the Parkway's 469 miles into a nearly 600-mile
mountain experience.

From Rockfish Gap (Milepost 0) to US 220 in Roanoke, Virginia (Milepost 121.4), the dramatically spinelike
ridge offers what some other sections of the high road
don't—views from towering forested peaks into valleys
checkerboarded with farms. These summits are largely
unsettled; national forests wrap the Parkway corridor in
multi-hundred thousand–acre woodlands. In the evening
these dark shapes bulk mysteriously against the twinkling of
valley towns far below.

The ridge is high and airy until Otter Creek (Mileposts
55–64), when the Parkway dips through intimate forests to

its lowest point—the James River, at 650 feet. Then up it climbs again, past the James River Face Wilderness and the high road's northern high point—3,950 feet, near Apple Orchard Mountain. Next are the Peaks of Otter's famous summits. From there it's a long scenic slide into the Roanoke Valley.

The Parkway's homage to the culture and history of the Southern highlands includes wayside exhibits and visitor centers. That starts immediately at Humpback Rocks Visitor Center and on the Mountain Farm Trail (typical late-1800s mountaineer farm). Don't miss this cultural side of the Parkway—trails are integral to its interpretation. Major interpretive sites include the James River Water Gap canal exhibit and Peaks of Otter's early-twentieth-century mountain farm and mid-1800s inn, Polly Woods Ordinary.

Parkway service sites include a restaurant at Otter Creek. Peaks of Otter Lodge is a highly regarded, spectacularly scenic spot to spend the night (even in winter, if you like to hike in the snow or cross-country ski). Campgrounds are also available at Otter Creek, Peaks of Otter, and Roanoke Mountain.

The USDA Forest Service Sherando Lake Recreation Area is a premier base for campers near the start of the road. Just across the Parkway from there, Wintergreen Mountain Resort represents the upscale end of the recreation and lodging experience. It's one of the South's premier ski areas and usually rated among the country's top tennis and golf resorts (with its own extensive trail system).

Anchoring the north and south of this section of the Parkway are cities worth a pause. The shaded sophistication of Charlottesville is on the north end, with the University of Virginia and an up-and-coming wine-producing region named after Thomas Jefferson's nearby home, Monticello. Near Lynchburg, Jefferson's summer home, Poplar Forest, is also open. Roanoke has its urban amenities, but a historic farmers' market is noteworthy.

Take the time to sample other cities and towns along this part of the Parkway—great attractions are within easy reach. There's the Frontier Culture Museum in Staunton. Civil War history saturates the Shenandoah Valley, and the Virginia Military Institute is just one of Lexington's attractions. Other sites honor George C. Marshall, "Stonewall" Jackson, and Robert E. Lee. There's historic downtown lodging at the Alexander-Withrow House and McCampbell Inn.

Natural Bridge, which Jefferson once owned, is still near the town of the same name. The offbeat free attraction Foamhenge—yes, a life-size replica made of foam—is just to the west on US 11. Bedford, just east of Peaks of Otter, is the site of the National D-Day Memorial. The town lost more soldiers per capita during the invasion than any other place in the country.

The first section of the Parkway will leave you wanting much more of these mountains. Luckily, there's 350 more miles to go.

1 Mountain Farm Trail (Milepost 5.8)

This trail offers an eye-opening glimpse into the rustic lives led by nineteenth-century Appalachian mountaineers who lived near what is now the Parkway.

Parkway milepost: 5.8
Distance: 0.5 mile out and back
Difficulty: Easy (wheelchair accessible)
Elevation gain: Negligible

Maps: *USGS Sherando;* Parkway map available at visitor center or www.nps.gov/blri/planyourvisit/brochures.htm

Finding the trailhead: Park at the visitor center and take the paved sidewalk south (left when facing the building).

The Hike

What a difference a century or so makes. The cabins and outbuildings of the re-created William J. Carter farm—not to mention seasonal programs and costumed interpreters—give startling insight into the lives of Appalachian mountaineers. This pioneering lifestyle still existed in some places when the Blue Ridge Parkway was built in the mid-1930s. The 1890s farm found on the Mountain Farm Trail isn't the original; it was re-created in 1950 using period structures. Nevertheless, it is an authentic setting explored by a very easy trail.

Buy the trail's inexpensive brochure at the visitor center and take the paved sidewalk that becomes a gravel lane (likely a section of a historic old turnpike you'll encounter on a loop of Humpback Rocks). On the left, you first reach a cabin and chicken house and then a "gear loft," where

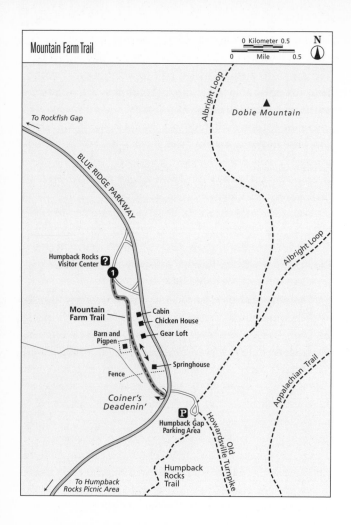

Mountain Farm Trail

0 Kilometer 0.5
0 Mile 0.5
N

To Rockfish Gap

BLUE RIDGE PARKWAY

Albright Loop

Dobie Mountain

Albright Loop

Humpback Rocks
Visitor Center ? 1

**Mountain
Farm Trail**

Cabin
Chicken House
Gear Loft

Barn and
Pigpen

Springhouse

Fence

*Coiner's
Deadenin'*

Appalachian Trail

P
Humpback Gap
Parking Area

Old Howardsville Turnpike

To Humpback
Rocks Picnic Area

Humpback
Rocks
Trail

the family stored their "plunder" (supplies and equipment). Past those structures and across the lane, a contorted barn is surrounded by a stone-walled pigpen. Farther on, a springhouse channels cold water through a sheltered food storage structure. Beyond that is "kissin' gate"; pass through and you're in "Coiner's Deadenin'," grass-covered meadows under the towering crag of Humpback Rocks. Here mountaineers cleared fields the slow way—by girdling the trees to kill them and planting crops between the leafless giants (which were later felled).

You can walk beyond the gate, gradually rising to Humpback Gap and trailhead parking for the Humpback Rocks Trail on the opposite side of the Parkway. Retrace your steps, or park at Humpback Rocks trailhead and take both trails from one central spot.

The steep trail to Humpback Rocks lifts hikers to truly awe-inspiring vistas that stretch north and south along the Blue Ridge, east to the Piedmont, and west into the Shenandoah Valley. It's a 1.0-mile climb on a blue-blazed trail that, though strenuous, has a partially gravel surface and resting benches along the way. When the gravel trail levels off at the top of a long uphill section, do not turn left—stay straight to be sure you're on the formal trail. That trail climbs wood and stone steps to a sign at the top where a left leads to the rocks. Past this sign, be sure to continue bearing left to reach the rocks—informal paths wander everywhere in this area. As you exit the rocks and re-enter the woods, bear to the right back up to the sign and the trail you came in on (it is easy to be drawn left and downhill on an old route that is sure to get you lost).

2 Greenstone Self-Guiding Trail (Milepost 8.8)

Take this twenty-minute self-guiding loop trail to learn about the geology of the northern Blue Ridge and see how mountaineers used their most abundant resource—rock—to wrest a living from harsh surroundings.

Parkway milepost: 8.8
Total distance: 0.2-mile loop
Difficulty: Easy

Maps: USGS Sherando; no Parkway map

Finding the trailhead: Park at the end of the overlook near the woods.

The Hike

Signs on this engaging self-guiding interpretive trail explain the natural setting and alerts you to the telltale signs of human habitation that are a stirring subtext to the Parkway experience.

The Mountain Farm Trail's extensive living-history exhibits re-create the picturesque side of the rustic Appalachian lifestyle. The Greenstone Trail imparts an anthropologist's insight into how to detect the evidence of a former mountain farm.

The overlook's interpretive sign explains that "hog walls" were scattered many places in the mountains. Built in the early 1800s and maintained in the winter by slaves from lower elevation plantations (Thomas Jefferson's Monticello is only 40 miles away), the walls penned nearly wild hogs that otherwise were permitted to roam the mast-covered slopes, becoming "free-range" delicacies. Before you hit the trail, look over the front of the overlook. Whether by accident or sensitivity, the builders of the Parkway spared the hog walls below, and the Park Service's vista maintenance crews periodically expose them to view.

Pass the trailhead sign and go right along the gravel path. A sign describes the ubiquitous green rock of the overlook and the general area—Catoctin greenstone—as an ancient lava flow, evidence that volcanoes once existed in the region. Were the lava to liquefy today, says the sign, it would fill the Shenandoah Valley. Undulating over occasional steps, the trail bears left around the end of the loop and across a dome of greenstone. Mountain laurel and Virginia pine cling to this steepening side of the ridge.

Pause at the sign that describes how tremendous earth forces 200 million years ago uplifted the lava, sandstone, limestone, and shale of the area, transforming it into ridges and peaks. Between Mileposts 20 and 60, the shale and limestone are particularly visible in road cuts—a favorite haunt for geology students touring the Parkway. At that sign, look to your right and behind, just below where the trail crosses the crag, and you'll see another hog wall—this one quite disheveled—arcing down through the rough woods. The sure of foot could go down and, being careful not to dislodge or alter the rocks, explore this high-mountain holding pen from centuries ago.

Swinging right, squeeze between a pine and a crag and emerge onto an open ledge with great views of the Shenandoah Valley. The vista here, as well was on the nearby Catoctin Trail in the Humpback Rocks Picnic Area at

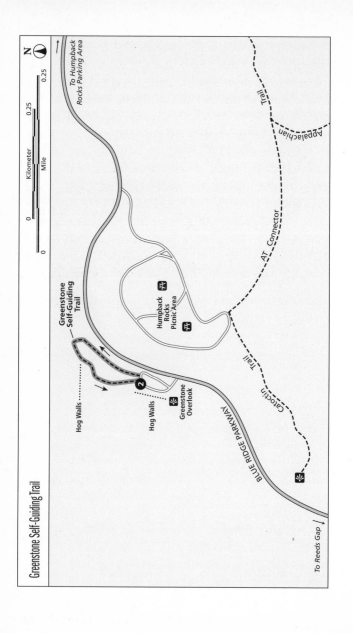

Greenstone Self-Guiding Trail

To Humpback Rocks Parking Area

N

Kilometer
0   0.25
0   0.25
Mile

Greenstone
Self-Guiding
Trail

Hog Walls

2

Hog Walls

Greenstone Overlook

Humpback Rocks Picnic Area

AT Connector

Appalachian Trail

Catoctin Trail

BLUE RIDGE PARKWAY

To Reeds Gap

Milepost 8.5 (another highly recommended easy trail—see the map), and at the clifftop Raven's Roost Overlook at Milepost 10.7, showcases the outstanding pastoral scenery that recommends this first part of the Parkway. When the leaves are off the trees, look ahead to the opposing ridge and notice the huge greenstone outcrops—like the one you're on—off in the woods.

Descending a flight of stone steps, the trail then rises over more steps past a crag where kids might hop off left into a greenstone cleft. An interpretive sign notes that you'll see all three types of rock along the Parkway—igneous (greenstone and lava), metamorphic (quartzite and schist), and sedimentary (limestone and sandstone). The trail climbs through a crag, to the right, and back into the parking lot.

3 Crabtree Falls (Milepost 27.2)

One of the South's best waterfall walks also has barrier-free access.

Parkway milepost: 27.2
Distance: 6.0-mile trail offers shorter out-and-back hikes from upper and lower trailheads. Turn around at Upper falls for 3.4-mile hike from bottom trailhead or 2.6-mile hike from upper trailhead.
Difficulty: More challenging from the bottom of the falls, moderate from the top

Elevation gain: 1,500 feet for the entire falls trail from the bottom; 1,000 feet to falls from the bottom; 500 feet to falls from the top
Maps: *USGS Montebello and Massies Mill; Appalachian Trail Conference: Pedlar Ranger District, George Washington National Forest;* Parkway map available online at www.nps.gov/blri/planyourvisit/brochures.htm

Finding the trailheads: Exit the Parkway at Milepost 27.2 and descend east on VA 56 for 6.6 miles to the lower trailhead on the right side of the road.

The upper trailhead is on VA 826, an unpaved road suitable for use in good weather by higher clearance vehicles (an SUV is the best choice). To reach that trailhead, go east on VA 56 from the Blue Ridge Parkway; in about 3.8 miles turn right onto VA 826. The upper trailhead is on the left in just under 4 miles.

The Hike

This Crabtree Falls isn't the last cataract you'll encounter with that name while driving south on the Blue Ridge Parkway. This Virginia hike is in George Washington National Forest. The second is actually a Blue Ridge Parkway trail—a strenuous 2.5-mile hike in North Carolina at Milepost 339.5.

Various publications describe Crabtree Falls as the "highest in Eastern America," the "highest in Virginia," and the "highest in the Virginia Blue Ridge." Which of those claims to believe probably depends on a long list of qualifiers and arguable assumptions. Chances are they at least qualify for "highest in the Virginia Blue Ridge" status—and that's being conservative.

Suffice to say that this path follows Crabtree Creek's 1,800 feet of descent to the Tye River. Along the way, five major waterfalls create a truly spectacular cascade.

Starting at VA 56, hikers are in for a climb, but this trail is highly developed and gradual over its entire length. The most recent renovation includes a seventy-car parking area, new barrier-free restrooms, and an approach that provides barrier-free access to the first overlook on the falls. The trail's improvements are largely designed to keep hikers away from the cascades, which have claimed more than twenty lives. Stay on the trail, and watch children closely.

Developed observation areas overlook the falls at four places along the trail, the first just above the parking area on the new trail. There's a wood deck overlook at 0.7 mile, and at 0.8 mile you can use a small cave to rejoin the trail above. An overlook at 1.4 miles looks up at the upper falls. The last overlook, at about 1.7 miles, surveys the Tye River Valley from above the upper falls. A return from that point makes a nice 3.4-mile out-and-back hike.

Continuing, the trail follows a gradual old grade and at 3.0 miles reaches an upper trailhead on VA 826. Keep this trailhead in mind for summer and fall weekends, when the lower trailhead may be jammed. The upper cascade is actu-

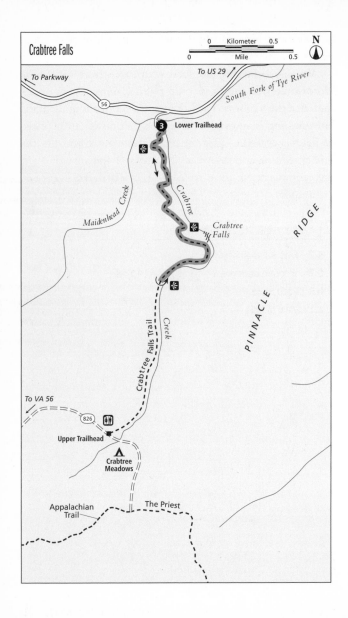

Crabtree Falls

0 — Kilometer — 0.5
0 — Mile — 0.5

N

To Parkway

To US 29

South Fork of Tye River

56

3 Lower Trailhead

Maidenhead Creek

Crabtree Creek

Crabtree Falls

RIDGE

Crabtree Falls Trail

Creek

PINNACLE

To VA 56

826

Upper Trailhead

Crabtree Meadows

Appalachian Trail

The Priest

ally an easier hike starting from the top. With two cars, a descent of the trail is an easy walk.

VA 826, a bumpy dirt road with easy stream fords, is a worthwhile side trip in its own right. Camping is not permitted at the Crabtree Falls Trail trailhead or along the trail, but camping is allowed in Crabtree Meadows, an expanse of fields across the split-rail fence from the trailhead and privies. The area looks exactly like what it was as recently as the early twentieth century—the rustic setting for a sawmill community.

Key Points from VA 56 Trailhead

0.2 First waterfall overlook.

0.7 Wooden deck overlook on second cascade.

0.8 Cave route.

1.7 View of falls.

4 **Yankee Horse Overlook Trail (Milepost 34.4)**

This is a quintessential Parkway leg-stretcher trail. Great views of Wigwam Falls combine with an interesting exhibit about the logging railroads that carried off the region's virgin timber.

Parkway milepost: 34.4
Distance: 0.1 to 0.2 mile out and back

Difficulty: Easy
Maps: *USGS Montebello;* no Parkway map

Finding the trailhead: Start on the right side of the overlook, by the interpretive sign.

The Hike

Blue Ridge Parkway interpretive trails impart an amazing sense of how people affected the mountain environment. If you open yourself to the insights, you'll start noticing the remains of old cabin sites and stone walls where you'd least expect them. This hike will change the way you look at trails wherever you hike in the eastern United States.

Remnants of the virgin forests encountered by the colonists are rare in the Appalachians today. The last of that timber was carried away in the early twentieth century on narrow-gauge railroads that climbed into the most impassable places on grades excavated by hand and lifted over precipitous gorges on log trestles. This trail explores a section of railroad reconstructed on the actual grade used by

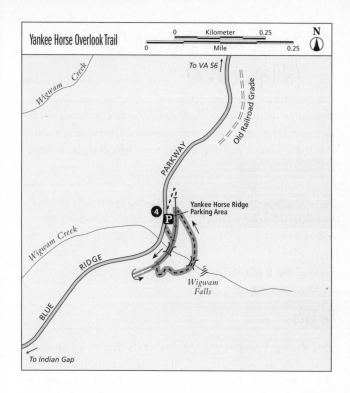

0   Kilometer   0.25

0   Mile   0.25

N

Wigwam Creek

To VA 56 ↑

Old Railroad Grade

PARKWAY

4 P   Yankee Horse Ridge Parking Area

Wigwam Creek

RIDGE

Wigwam Falls

BLUE

To Indian Gap

the Irish Creek Railway to transport more than 100 million board feet of lumber. Built in 1919 and 1920, the railway was 50 miles long.

Up stone steps, the trail rises and turns right onto railroad tracks across a log-supported bridge that spans gushing Wigwam Creek. The path goes left beyond the bridge, but don't turn yet. Follow the tracks as the rails end and the ties continue past a pile of huge timbers. When the ties stop, keep going a short distance and see how the grade softens and the woods encroach.

Many trails use portions of grades like this, and most hikers assume they're old farm or auto roads. Some of the grades you encounter on the Parkway, especially near gaps, may be wagon roads from centuries past. But many are railroad grades, and now you may be better able to recognize them. Drive north a short distance from this overlook; where the hillside recedes from the road on the right, you can see the continuation of this very railroad grade slicing through the woods.

Return to where you would have gone left and turn right (uphill). Pass a tree growing over a huge boulder on the right and then go left across two bridges below impressive Wigwam Falls. The trail continues left, levels above the stream, and then descends on a log-lined treadway to rejoin the tracks. Head left, back toward the bridge, and take a right to your car. Or go right on the tracks toward a picnic table and then left down steps to the overlook.

5 Otter Creek Trail and Otter Lake Loop (Mileposts 60.8–63.6)

Enjoy serene streamside strolling in a memorable mixed forest of hardwoods and evergreens. The Otter Creek Trail sticks close to the Parkway for its entire 3.5-mile length—three trailheads allow you to create your own hike. The route's terrain is so gentle that any distance qualifies as a moderate hike. You can also add a quick but scenic loop around Otter Lake to include a ruined mountaineer cabin; it also makes a great short hike by itself.

Parkway mileposts: 60.8 (campground), 63.1 (Otter Lake), and 63.6 (James River Visitor Center)
Distance: 3.5 miles one way from Otter Creek Campground to James River Visitor Center; 5.6 miles out and back from campground to Otter Lake Overlook; 1.6 miles out and back from visitor center to overlook. Adding Otter Lake loop makes a 6.4-mile hike to and from campground and 2.4 miles from visitor center.

Difficulty: Moderate
Elevation gain: For out-and-back hikes: 125 feet from campground, 30 feet from visitor center; including Otter Lake Loop, 222 feet from campground, 128 feet from visitor center.
Maps: *USGS Big Island;* Parkway map available in season at visitor center and campground and at www.nps.gov/blri/planyour visit/brochures.htm

Finding the trailheads: For the Otter Creek Trail, park at the restaurant (or nearby parking) and head south past the front of the building on the paved then gravel-surfaced trail that dips into the woods along the stream.

Starting at the James River Overlook, beside the visitor center, park near the trail map sign and descend to the right below the front of the building on the paved path. Turn left just beyond the visitor center and follow the paved path above the picnic tables and down into the woods.

For just the Otter Lake Loop, park at the Otter Lake Overlook.

The Hikes

From Otter Creek Campground

The Otter Creek Trail leaves the parking area and immediately passes circular concrete stepping-stones that cross the stream left into the campground. (You'll see more of these 1950s-looking conveniences all along the trail.) Passing campsites, the trail crosses to the east side of the river at 0.1 mile and then slips under Otter Creek Bridge 6 at 0.3 mile and wanders west to stone steps that lead left up to Terrapin Hill Overlook at 0.6 mile (Milepost 61.4).

The trail swings south with the stream and goes under two bridges at 0.7 mile, both through the leftmost water tunnels. The Parkway's stone Otter Creek bridge 7 is followed by the concrete modernity of the VA 130 bridge. Just out of the tunnel, the trail turns right and crosses to the other side of the stream. Along the river rocks on the shore, the stream is deflected hard right by a towering green palisade; turn with it.

Paralleling VA 130, the trail again hops to the east side of the stream and rises steeply left to parallel above the Parkway (which has crossed above the other road). The path rises higher and higher along a log-lined treadway through an impressive forest of white oak, hemlock, and white pine to a bench at 1.0 mile. After a dip left into a dry drainage, the trail swings out again and back in to a bridge at 1.3

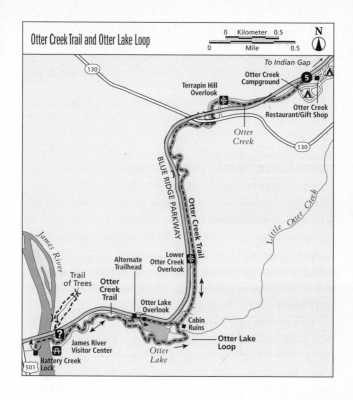

Otter Creek Trail and Otter Lake Loop

miles. Swinging into another drainage, then out, the trail is again above Otter Creek. Entering into another drainage, side steps lead to a huge crag with an overhanging shelter spot and a bench. Cross a scenic crag with a view below; the trail swings out and steeply down to Otter Creek at about 1.5 miles.

From here to Lower Otter Creek Overlook (Milepost 62.5) at 1.9 miles, the trail stays near the stream, barely undulating with nice views into clear, cold, and at times invitingly deep water. Mountain laurel crops up and you pass another bench. Entering the overlook's picnic area, take a right across the steel bridge, walk left along the parking area, and immediately go left across the next bridge (the zigzag avoids a cliff face).

Back along the stream, this time on a sandier shore, the Otter Creek Trail enters a more open deciduous forest and at 2.6 miles joins the Otter Lake Loop. Go right at this junction, crossing two steel bridges. Staying right, emerge from the woods to walk along the Otter Lake Overlook toward the dam (Milepost 63.1) at 2.8 miles, a 5.6-mile round-trip if you backtrack to the campground from here. This direction is the best way to circle the lake and is the Otter Lake Loop Trail described below (for 6.4-mile circuit back to the campground).

Key Points

0.3 Under first bridge.

0.6 Terrapin Hill Overlook.

0.7 Under second and third bridges.

1.9 Lower Otter Creek Overlook.

2.6 Junction with Otter Lake Loop.

2.8 Otter Lake Overlook.

5.6 Arrive back at campground (6.4 if you circle the lake).

From James River Visitor Center

Heading down to the woods line above the visitor center picnic area, leave the paved path and join Otter Creek. Here it's a quiet stream, backed up into stillness by the lumbering flow of the nearby James River. Soon, though, the stream comes to life as its rise creates a rush of incoming water.

Following the creek beneath the visitor center parking, the path runs atop a stone reinforcement wall at 0.3 mile that protects the road from the curving waters of Otter Creek. Across the stream, hemlocks grapple to stay rooted among mossy-green crags. The trail swings right then left around a bend in the river (where you can see evidence of an old road off to the left) and then crosses more round stepping-stones. The trail joins an old grade at 0.5 mile and leaves it at 0.6 mile to cross a small stream. This atmospheric evidence of early wagon roads and later logging railroads jibes with the chimneys and other ruins that the alert hiker will notice hereabouts.

This was a region of rich soil and impressive forests, and the Kanawha Canal—on the James, just 0.5 mile down Otter Creek—was one of early America's thriving commercial thoroughfares. Continuing through hemlocks, white pines, and a carpet of running cedar, the river straightens out and the trail dips down railroad tie steps to stepping-stones at 0.7 mile. Just beyond is the stair-stepping cascade of water over the Otter Lake dam.

You could cross the stream and walk up the steps beside the dam to the Otter Lake Overlook at 0.8 mile, then retrace your steps to the visitor center for a 1.6-mile round-trip. To include the lake, go right before the stepping-stones and start the Otter Lake Loop Trail (see below). Hiking the 1.0-mile lake trail and retracing your steps along Otter Creek to the James River Visitor Center creates a 2.4-mile circuit.

Otter Lake Loop

Either of the trails described above will bring you to the Otter Lake Overlook, from where you can start the lake loop. At the end of the Otter Lake Overlook near the dam, go down the steps and cross the concrete stepping-stones. Go left and ascend stone steps past crags along the stream and above the dam at 0.1 mile. At lake level, the trail slides around a point and into a drainage to cross a small stream, then switchbacks around the ridge to a bench above the lake at 0.3 mile. A small side trail leads to another view of the lake.

The main trail rises gradually to its high point in the mixed deciduous and evergreen forest. At 0.4 mile another bench amid towering white pines announces the drop down a gully from the ridgetop. Bearing left across a small creek, the trail wanders through sycamores and blond grasses in the wetland where inlet brooks feed the lake. Cross a small bridge at 0.5 mile over Little Otter Creek, and then rise into a white pine grove on a knoll where an old cabin sits in ruins. The huge base of the chimney is nicely intact, but the upper rocks have fallen in much the way the rocks originally were stacked, directly across the interior of the cabin. A perimeter of rock foundation stones and the remnants of large logs are all that's left. A bench is across the trail.

Dipping down into the floodplain below the once artfully sited cabin, turn left at the signed junction (a right takes you back to the campground if you started there) and cross two steel bridges at 0.6 mile. At the edge of the Parkway, head left. Rounding a ridge above the wetland, walk into the parking area, past a wooden observation deck on the lakeshore, and back to your car for a 1.0-mile loop. If you started at the visitor center, head down the steps by the dam, cross the stepping-stones, turn right and hike back downstream.

Note: The lake is plentifully signed with fishing regulations (swimming, boating, and ice-skating are prohibited).

Key Points

0.1 Cross stream and go left (a right leads to the visitor center) to top of dam.

0.3 First bench at side trail to view.

0.4 Second bench.

0.6 Turn left (a right leads to the campground) and cross bridges.

1.0 Arrive back at dam beside Parkway.

6 James River Trail/Trail of Trees (Milepost 63.6)

A pleasant walk across a scenic river bridge leads to a self-guiding interpretive exhibit at a canal lock built in the mid-1800s.

Parkway milepost: 63.6
Total distance: James River Trail, 0.4 mile out and back; Trail of Trees, 0.5-mile loop
Difficulty: Easy

Maps: *USGS Big Island;* Parkway map available in season at visitor center and campground and at www.nps.gov/blri/planyour visit/brochures.htm

Finding the trailhead: Park at the visitor center and descend to the right on the paved path from the trail map sign. Continue straight in front of the visitor center and turn left under the Blue Ridge Parkway's river bridge and take the pedestrian walkway left across the river.

The Hikes

James River Trail

The James River Trail crosses the impressive pedestrian span beneath the Blue Ridge Parkway bridge. Descend the steps on the west side of the river and go left across the grassy riverside meadow to Battery Creek Lock. Built in 1848 and used between 1851 and 1880 on the James River and Kanawha Canal, the lock lifted and lowered boats around part of the river's 13 feet of drop from nearby Buchanan, a Shenandoah Valley town and western terminus of the canal.

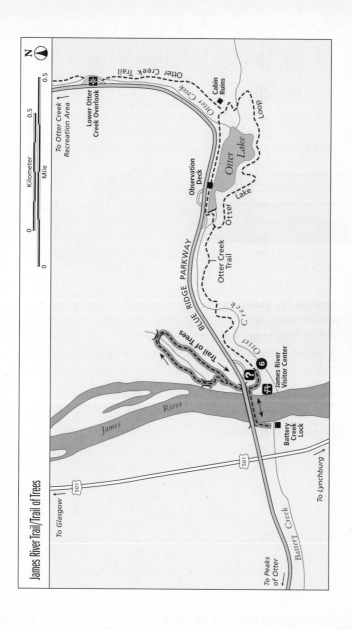

James River Trail/Trail of Trees

To Glasgow
501
To Peaks of Otter
To Lynchburg
501
Battery Creek

James River
River

Battery Creek Lock
James River Visitor Center
Trail of Trees
Otter Creek
BLUE RIDGE PARKWAY
Otter Creek Trail
Observation Deck
Otter Lake
Otter Lake Loop
Cabin Ruins
Otter Creek Trail
Otter Creek
Lower Otter Creek Overlook
To Otter Creek Recreation Area

N

Kilometer
0   0.5
0   0.5
Mile

Signs interpret the lock and the system that used river water to feed the adjoining canal and operate its gates.

To lengthen the walk, go beyond the lock to the river or walk along the creek before returning to the bridge on the way back.

Key Points

0.2   Battery Creek Lock.

Trail of Trees

The moderate 0.5-mile Trail of Trees loop branches right just before the pedestrian bridge (left on the way back). The trail interprets the riverside forest and the distinctive geology of this "water gap."

7 Abbott Lake Trail (Milepost 85.6)

One of the Parkway's best lakeside strolls or cross-country ski tours adjoins Peaks of Otter Lodge.

Parkway milepost: 85.6
Distance: 1.0-mile loop around Abbott Lake; 1.6 miles round-trip from picnic area, 1.7 miles from visitor center
Difficulty: Easy
Elevation gain: Negligible

Maps: *USGS Peaks of Otter;* Parkway map available at visitor center (in season), lodge, and other Parkway facilities and online at www.nps.gov/blri/planyourvisit/brochures.htm

Finding the trailheads: To park at Peaks of Otter Lodge, turn into the lodge and take the next right into the small lakeshore parking area by the first building. At busier times of year you may have to park elsewhere in the lodge lot and take a paved path to the lakeshore.

For a longer walk, start at either Peaks of Otter Picnic Area on US 43 or the Peaks of Otter Visitor Center on the Parkway. To start at the picnic area, turn east onto US 43 opposite the visitor center. Take the next left into the picnic area. At the T junction, park across the road at the Flat Top Trail Parking Area or go left and park closer to Polly Woods Ordinary. You can also park at the visitor center on the path north to the Johnson Farm and take the right under the Parkway to Peaks of Otter Lodge.

The Hike

Abbott Lake is the centerpiece of the 4,200-acre Peaks of Otter Recreation Area, one of the Parkway's most highly recommended places to spend a day or stop for the night.

Peaks of Otter Lodge, on the shore of Abbott Lake, is one of four concessionaire-operated accommodations on the Parkway. It is open year-round for lodging and dining, with special buffets on Friday night and Sunday. Other facilities operated May through October by the Park Service include a campground, picnic area, country store, nature center, and visitor center.

The lake was once a high-elevation mountain bog and a favored Native American hunting area—elk, bison, and other game were attracted to the watery site. European settlers first cleared the land in 1766; by the 1830s an "ordinary" was established that offered lodging and dining to travelers crossing the Blue Ridge. Early tourist hotels, ancestors of the current Peaks of Otter Lodge, opened as early as 1857.

Today the lake still attracts plentiful wildlife. This is a great place for bird-watching—if you can divert your eyes from the knock-your-socks-off view of Sharp Top. The peak, topping out at 3,875 feet, is so close and conical that the view is truly dramatic—especially if you factor in atmospherics or such seasonal spectacles as autumn color or hoarfrost in the colder months. That's great for very young, elderly, and even hikers with limited mobility—not to mention cross-country skiers—because this trail is also partially paved and extremely easy (hence suggested starting points that add to the distance).

The best starting point is the picnic area. Go left up the picnic area road past Big Spring, a reliable water source used for centuries by travelers traversing the Blue Ridge. Take the path past Polly Woods Ordinary, a modest cabin used as a rustic inn by owner Mary "Polly" Woods between 1830 and 1855. Appropriately, given your destination, the building was originally located up near the lake and served travelers on the Buchanan to Liberty (early name of Bedford, Virginia) Turnpike.

In 0.3 mile you'll turn right onto the paved Abbott Lake Trail and head northwest along the lakeshore. Cross an arched bridge at 0.4 mile and veer out into the lake on a promontory with benches and great views. Past the lodge, the pavement ends and a trail branches right at 0.7 mile to pass under the Parkway and then left on its way in about 0.4 mile to the visitor center (another good starting point).

Continuing, the now unpaved path wanders at the water's edge along the Parkway through open meadows dotted with dogwoods, cedars, and cattails. You'll cross the inlet brook on a bridge at 0.9 mile and pass a trail to Peaks of Otter Campground at 1.1 miles. (Campers can come in from this direction; campground trails link the campsites to Abbott Lake, the start of the Sharp Top Trail, and the visitor center.) Cross the dam and at 1.3 miles turn right past Polly Woods Ordinary along the picnic area that you came in on. Back at your car, the round-trip is about 1.6 miles.

From the visitor center, hike 0.3 mile toward Johnson Farm to a trail junction. The Johnson Farm Trail loops left, but take the right toward the lodge and go beneath the road via an underpass. Turn right at the Abbott Lake Trail. This route is about 1.7 miles.

If the stunning views of Sharp Top entice you to head to the summit, the 1.5-mile strenuous hike to the top starts opposite the Peaks of Otter Visitor Center beside the Nature Center. During the summer season, a National Park Service shuttle bus ferries riders to the summit of Sharp Top for a small fee, making it easy for people to hike down who might not otherwise make the climb up (ask about current rates

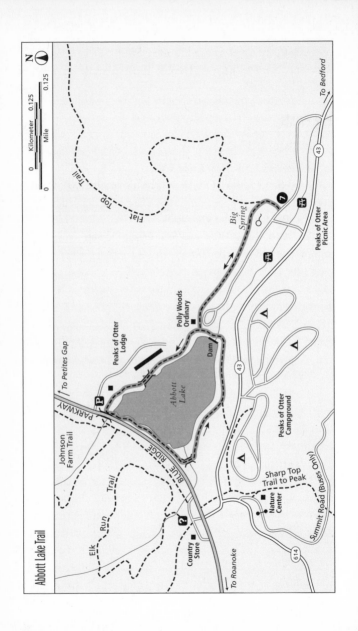

Abbott Lake Trail

N

0   Kilometer   0.125

0   Mile   0.125

To Bedford

43

7

Peaks of Otter Picnic Area

Big Spring

Flat Top Trail

Polly Woods Ordinary

Peaks of Otter Lodge

Dam

Abbott Lake

To Petites Gap

PARKWAY

P

BLUE RIDGE

Johnson Farm Trail

Elk Run Trail

?

Country Store

Peaks of Otter Campground

Sharp Top Trail to Peak

Nature Center

Summit Road (Buses Only)

43

614

To Roanoke

and departure times at the Country Store or visitor center). Even though this hike is steep, it is often made by families and older persons.

Key Points

0.0 Peaks of Otter Picnic Area.

0.3 Turn right onto Abbott Lake Trail.

0.7 Trail to Johnson Farm Trail and visitor center branches to the right.

0.9 Cross bridge over inlet brook.

1.3 Turn right to trailhead past Polly Woods Ordinary.

8 Johnson Farm, Harkening Hill, and Elk Run Loop Trails (Milepost 85.9)

These scenic, short to moderate-length interpretive trails impart a real sense of how Southern Appalachian mountaineers lived. A 3.9-mile outer loop of the Johnson Farm and Harkening Hill Trails rolls the human and natural history of the area into one wonderful walk.

Parkway milepost: 85.9
Distance: 2.1 miles out and back for Johnson Farm; circuits of 3.3 and 3.9 miles for Harkening Hill; 0.8-mile loop for Elk Run Loop Trail
Difficulty: Easy to moderate for Johnson Farm; more challenging for Harkening Hill; easy for Elk Run Loop Trail
Elevation gain: 814 feet for Harkening Hill
Maps: *USGS Peaks of Otter;* Parkway map available at visitor center (in season), lodge, and other Parkway facilities and online at www.nps.gov/blri/planyourvisit/brochures.htm

Finding the trailhead: These three interconnected loops start at the Peaks of Otter Visitor Center.

The Hike

The Harkening Hill, Johnson Farm, and Elk Run Interpretive Loop Trails are interconnected, which creates an interesting situation: You can be on a section of two different hikes at once. All hikes are best started from the Peaks of Otter Visitor Center. Together or separately, they offer insight into the lifestyle of Southern Appalachian mountaineers.

By the 1930s a community of more than twenty self-reliant families populated this high valley under Sharp Top, including the last of the Johnson family, for whom the Johnson Farm Trail is named. A school and a church stood near the current site of the Peaks of Otter Lodge (built in 1964). The families were mostly subsistence farmers, but the tourist traffic to the hotel and up the road to the Sharp Top summit supplied cash for the locals who had jobs.

The Great Depression ended all that. The Johnson Farm, which got its start in 1852, was sold in 1941, changed hands again, and was then purchased by the National Park Service. It deteriorated until the 1950s, when it was stabilized; it was restored in 1968. The interpretive Johnson Farm Loop Trail is one of the best places on the Parkway to learn about the lives of the people who wrested subsistence from the rocky Appalachian soil. Warm-weather living-history programs here are among the Parkway's most engaging and extensive.

The easy-to-moderate Johnson Farm hike starts at the northern end of the visitor center parking lot. Take the scenic roadside path toward Peaks of Otter Lodge and reach a trail junction in about 0.3 mile. The first trail to the left is the return part of the Johnson Farm loop. Take a left at the second sign—the farm is closer that way—and head out into the grassy meadow. (The trail that goes right leads under the Parkway to the lodge and Abbott Lake.)

Bear right in the meadow along the trees past a sign about the Hotel Mons, the post–Polly Woods Ordinary/ pre–Peaks of Otter Lodge summer resort that operated here from 1857 to the late 1930s. Pass a trail sign farther down the meadow and enter the woods at a small bridge. The trail rises and goes left on a road grade into the farm at just under 1.0 mile from the parking area.

Leave the old Johnson place one of two ways. The easier walk is to retrace your steps for a 2.1-mile round-trip. Or leave the house past the front porch and crop plantings and head uphill and left into the meadow beyond to the Johnson Farm return trail. At 1.3 miles the return trail goes straight at a junction where the Harkening Hill Trail turns right. (Go right for a 3.9-mile perimeter loop formed by the Johnson Farm and Harkening Hill Trails.)

Stay on the Johnson Farm Trail and descend to the first junction you passed at the start of the hike. A right there returns to the visitor center in just more than 2.0 miles.

The longest walk is the Harkening Hill Trail, either 3.3 miles (going left at the first sign from the visitor center on the Johnson Farm Trail) or about 3.9 miles (via the longer outer loop of Johnson Farm). This trail explores the now wooded, wildflower-filled forest that eighty years ago was cultivated fields and road grades between the Johnson Farm and the peak directly above it—Harkening Hill (3,364 feet). The hike is rated more challenging, but it's only moderately so—800 feet of elevation gain over roughly 2.0 miles from either direction.

The Johnson Farm loop affords the best start for this hike by adding human context to a setting returning to nature. Whichever side of the farm loop you start on, branch off on the Harkening Hill Trail. You'll pass through two small meadows at 0.5 mile. A side trail to Balance Rock, a boulder perched on a natural pedestal, heads left at about 0.7 mile.

At 0.8 mile above your turnoff, you've slipped onto national forest land to the limited rocky viewpoint of Harkening Hill (2.1 miles via the right-hand side of the Johnson Farm loop; 1.6 miles on the left). The trail then undulates down the broad, boulder-strewn summit ridge through scenic open woods with a number of descents, some of them steep. There's a sharp ridgeline and grass-fringed uphill a

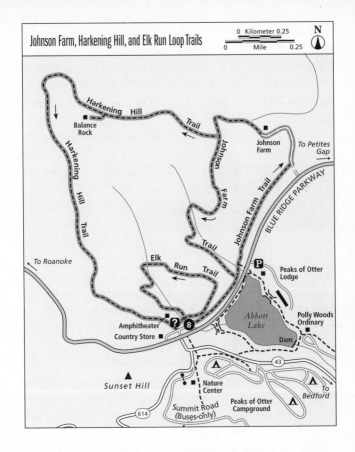

0 Kilometer 0.25
0 Mile 0.25

N

Harkening Hill Trail

Balance Rock

Johnson Farm Trail

Johnson Farm

To Petites Gap

Harkening Hill Trail

BLUE RIDGE PARKWAY

To Roanoke

Elk Run Trail

P

Peaks of Otter Lodge

Amphitheater
Country Store

? 8

Abbott Lake

Polly Woods Ordinary

Dam

43

Sunset Hill

Nature Center

Peaks of Otter Campground

To Bedford

614

Summit Road (Buses only)

mile below the peak—3.1 miles from the visitor center via
the right leg of the Johnson Farm Trail, 2.6 miles via the left.
The trail descends by switchbacks and then right between
the rows of amphitheater seats and through the visitor center
breezeway at 3.9 miles (3.3 miles using the left leg).

The shortest hike in the three-trail network near the
Peaks of Otter Visitor Center is the easy 0.8-mile Elk Run

Loop Trail, which starts in the breezeway at the end of the Harkening Hill loop. The interpretive signs of this educational nature trail tell of the ecological interaction between plants and animals. Following the signs through the gap in the visitor center, bear right and come to the first of many benches in 0.1 mile. An old grade becomes the path on its rise to a cemetery at 0.7 mile, before dipping back to the visitor center.

Key Points on the Longer Circuit

0.3 Take the second left on the Johnson Farm Trail.

1.0 Johnson Farm.

1.3 Turn right onto the Harkening Hill Trail.

2.0 Trail to Balance Rock.

2.1 Summit of Harkening Hill.

2.6 Good view on the way down.

The Blue Ridge Plateau

Mileposts 121.4 (US 220 at Roanoke, Virginia) to 276.4 (US 421 at Deep Gap, North Carolina)

The 155-mile portion of the Parkway from US 220 in Roanoke (Milepost 121.4) to Deep Gap at US 421 (Milepost 276.4) could be considered two sections if you split it at the Virginia–North Carolina state line. I-77 is a nice central access point near the middle.

Both of these subsections share a common flavor. This is where the Appalachian Front undulates south from Roanoke at generally lower elevations to the Virginia line, then rises again in North Carolina. To the east, the Piedmont still lies below—just not as far below—and western views don't generally plummet to deep valleys. This is the Blue Ridge Plateau of rolling uplands, farms, and rural communities—a bucolic side of the Southern Appalachians.

Unlike other parts of the Parkway, here public lands don't lie beyond the National Park boundary. Residential and, increasingly, resort development are more visible.

Groups such as the Blue Ridge Parkway Foundation and Friends of the Blue Ridge Parkway are working closely with the Park Service to minimize the impact of what hikers would call "development" but residents of Appalachia often call "economic opportunity." For many of them, that opportunity has been a long time coming.

Fittingly, this part of the road is where human habitation of the mountains and the culture of the mountain people truly seem to stand out. This part may come closest to fusing the Parkway's interpretation of the past with a sense of the present and future.

You'll see the Parkway's pioneer cabins and structures everywhere (most often on the trails in this book) and even "meet" some of the people who lived in them. Mabry Mill; Cool Springs Baptist Church; and Mathews, Trails, Puckett, Brinegar, Caudill, and Jesse Brown Cabins stand like silent portals to the past. Not all are exhibits. As you motor by, you may not even glimpse Sheets Cabin standing alone below the road at Milepost 252.3—with no nearby parking lot. You'll see fences too, especially at the Groundhog Mountain exhibit. During the season, living-history interpreters movingly personify this "land of do without" lifestyle.

You'll see historic structures when you hike into Rock Castle Gorge (Milepost 167) or the backcountry of Doughton Park (Milepost 239), but there's more. You'll see where fields are becoming forests again. You'll see nature reclaiming a hardscrabble landscape where people struggled for generations attempting to make a living. Rock walls and stone chimneys are their monuments.

The people who lived here are gone now, but their progeny work or own businesses in tourism and other industries, including Christmas tree farms, that you'll see all around you. They display their crafts at the Northwest Trading Post (Milepost 258.7), and traditional mountain music—so recently resurgent as a part of the country music scene—is featured stunningly in one of the Parkway's newest facilities, Blue Ridge Music Center (Milepost 213). Extensive exhibits complement the center's in-season schedule of popular outdoor concerts. Not far off the road, from Galax, Virginia (the Old Time Fiddler's Convention, second weekend in August), to Wilkesboro, North Carolina (MerleFest, last weekend of April), real music events still do what they've always done—tempt people, including Parkway tourists, out of the hollows.

The long list of major Parkway service sites on this 155-mile stretch include Smart View Picnic Area (Milepost 154.5), Rocky Knob Campground (Milepost 167.1) and Picnic Area (Milepost 169), Mabry Mill (Milepost 176.2), and Groundhog Mountain Picnic Area (Milepost 188.8)—and those are just to the Virginia–North Carolina state line at Milepost 216.9.

In North Carolina, Cumberland Knob Picnic Area is where Parkway construction started (Milepost 217.5). Doughton Park is next, with a campground (Milepost 239.2), accommodations at Bluffs Lodge, a restaurant, and picnic area (Milepost 241.1).

With so much private land along the road, this section has a wealth of smaller roads that come and go. Take a chance and explore a few of the public ones. There are surprises. The mountain town of Floyd, Virginia (Mileposts 158.9 and 159.3), is a destination on "The Crooked Road, Virginia Music Heritage Trail"—a 250-mile drive that crosses the Parkway and includes the Blue Ridge Music Center. There's great atmosphere and live music at Floyd Country Store. Tours and tastings at nearby Chateau Morrissette (Milepost 171.5) give a nod to the growing Blue

Ridge regional wine industry—with a reliable restaurant and vintages produced on premises.

The Mayberry Trading Post (Milepost 180.5) and the cluster of services at Fancy Gap (Milepost 199.4) are enjoyably oriented to tourism.

⑨ Rock Castle Gorge Day Hike (Milepost 165.3)

A streamside exploration of a scenic valley in the Rocky Knob Recreation Area imparts a startling sense of what life was like for early-twentieth-century mountain residents.

Parkway milepost: 165.3
Distance: 10.6-mile Rock Castle Gorge Trail for out-and-back hikes of 3.0, 4.8, and 5.4 miles
Difficulty: Easy to more challenging
Elevation gain: 1,050 feet for the out-and-back hike to the stone chimney
Maps: *USGS Woolwine;* Parkway map available at visitor center (in season) and other facilities and online at www.nps.gov/blri/planyourvisit/brochures.htm

Finding the trailhead: To start the Rock Castle Gorge Trail near the backcountry campsite, go east on VA 8 from Tuggle Gap (Milepost 165.3) and turn right at the bottom of the hill onto VA 605. Park at the end of this dirt road.

The Hikes

A day hike along Rock Castle Creek is one of the best ways to explore the Rocky Knob Recreation Area, a 3,589-acre backcountry bulge from the Parkway that contains a trail system extensive enough to permit backpack camping. You'll pass the campsite on this hike—it's an easy overnighter (permit required).

Rocky Knob boasts a wonderful mix of high-elevation meadows, craggy-summit views, deep coves, and poignant reminders that many a now-wild Appalachian wilderness

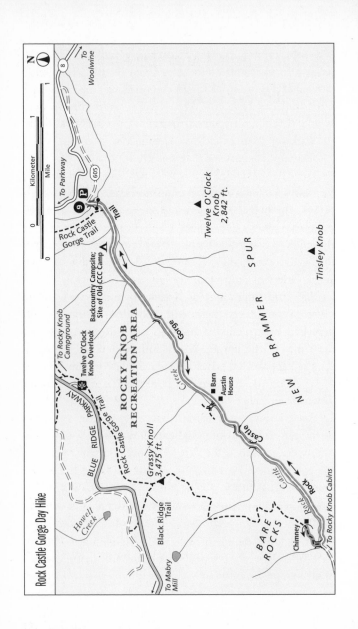

Rock Castle Gorge Day Hike

was once home to isolated mountaineer families. This hike passes a farmhouse from the days when Rock Castle Gorge contained a thriving community. You'll also pass a former Civilian Conservation Corps (CCC) camp that is now Rocky Knob's backcountry campsite. The CCC labored on the Parkway during the Great Depression.

Leaving the parking area on VA 605, cross the gated bridge. The green-blazed Rock Castle Gorge Trail wanders for nearly 3.0 miles ever higher up the valley. Almost immediately, the higher elevation side of the loop trail branches right and follows Little Rock Castle Creek. Staying left in the valley, a few short climbs reach a long streamside stretch that leads by the old CCC camp at 0.3 mile. There's a privy and a variety of campsites with grills and benches.

The road climbs in steps. Sycamores and copious quartz outcrops are everywhere (the six-sided quartz crystals prevalent here reminded residents of castle towers, hence the name of the gorge). A half mile above the campsite, the road appears less traveled. After the first stream crossing at 1.2 miles, the trail makes a brief climb then levels with downstream valley views.

At 1.5 miles you come upon a barn and an early-twentieth-century white clapboard house with a privy and outbuildings. This is the Austin House, the only home in the gorge today. Built in 1916, it was the finest house in a community of thirty-plus families. The population dwindled when wage-paying industries came to surrounding communities and undermined a lifestyle of subsistence farming. The farm is an eerie reminder of human transience—especially with jonquils announcing another spring in a long-untended garden.

Take the bridge across the creek for a picnic in the rough fields (remember, no camping is permitted here). A return from here is an easy to moderate 3.0-mile day hike.

Beyond the fields, the road rises steeply and repeatedly, with great views straight down on the creek. A gorge forms to the right, and the road continues steeply. At 2.4 miles Rock Castle Cascades splash off the cliffs and shower down to the left of the roadside. Turn around here for a more challenging 4.8-mile out-and-back hike.

The trail continues (there's a neat stone chimney not too much farther, for a round-trip of 5.4 miles) and eventually climbs across the crest of the Rocky Knob area before descending Little Rock Castle Creek back to your starting point to complete a more challenging 10.6-mile loop hike.

Key Points

- **0.3** CCC backcountry campsite.
- **1.2** Cross first bridge.
- **1.5** Arrive at the Austin House.
- **1.7** Cross second bridge and third bridge, 0.1 mile beyond.
- **2.4** Rock Castle Cascades shower left side of the trail.
- **2.6** Final bridge at bench.
- **2.7** Chimney at old homesite.
- **5.4** Arrive back at trailhead.

10 Rocky Knob Day Hike (Milepost 168.0)

A short hike takes you to Rocky Knob's signature summit.

Parkway milepost: 168.0
Distance: 1.1-mile loop
Difficulty: Easy to moderate
Elevation gain: 190 feet

Maps: *USGS Woolwine;* Parkway map available at visitor center and other facilities and online at www.nps.gov/blri/planyourvisit/brochures.htm

Finding the trailhead: The trail leaves the south end of Saddle Overlook.

The Hike

Rocky Knob's namesake summit is known for the area's best views, especially of Rock Castle Gorge. There is also a historical oddity—the shelter on the summit of Rocky Knob was an Appalachian Trail shelter before Parkway construction forced the trail far to the west.

Head south out of Saddle Overlook; when the green-blazed Rock Castle Gorge Trail goes left to climb the peak, bear right onto the easy, red-blazed side trail that avoids the summit. Another red-blazed side trail goes left, but stay right. In 0.5 mile turn left; the green-blazed trail climbs to the crest of the ridge and great views. Dipping through a swale on the crest, the path runs to the summit (3,572 feet) and the shelter at 0.9 mile. The path then dips off the peak, passes an intersection with the red-blazed linking trail,

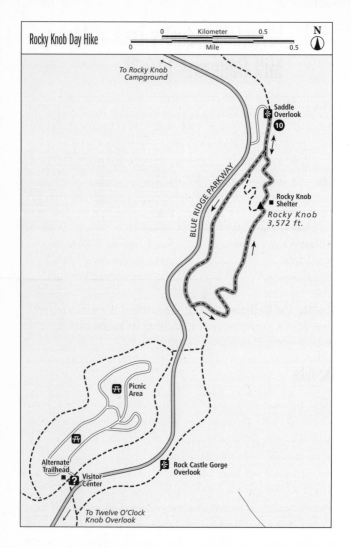

Rocky Knob Day Hike

0   Kilometer   0.5

0   Mile   0.5

N

To Rocky Knob
Campground

Saddle
Overlook
10

BLUE RIDGE PARKWAY

Rocky Knob
Shelter

*Rocky Knob
3,572 ft.*

Picnic
Area

Alternate
Trailhead

Visitor
Center

Rock Castle Gorge
Overlook

To Twelve O'Clock
Knob Overlook

rejoins the side trail you took past the peak, and returns to
Saddle Overlook at 1.1 miles.

11 Mountain Industry Trail at Mabry Mill (Milepost 176.2)

This highly developed and popular paved path (with wheelchair access) explores a virtual mountain community. Mabry Mill, probably the Parkway's most photographed site, is surrounded by historic structures and informative exhibits about the early Appalachian economy.

Parkway milepost: 176.2
Distance: 0.5-mile loop
Difficulty: Easy (wheelchair accessible)

Maps: *USGS Meadows of Dan;* Parkway map available in season at restaurant/gift shop and online at www.nps.gov/blri/planyourvisit/brochures.htm

Finding the trailhead: Parking is available at the restaurant/gift shop. Access to overflow parking lots is signed on the Parkway from both directions. (See the accompanying map.)

The Hike

How popular is this trail? One indication is that two Parkway trail maps are printed—one oriented from the restaurant/gift shop, the other from the overflow parking lot. Signs at those sites mirror the maps.

But don't let tour buses deter you. This trail features what is perhaps the Parkway's most photographed site, Mabry Mill—a scene notoriously claimed by postcards from states other than Virginia. A stop here also impresses with what is surely one of the more complex systems of water flumes ever devised to feed an otherwise primitive water-powered facility. Indeed, Mabry Mill and the blacksmith shop are no relocated historic structures, as some are along the Parkway. This is their original, if now landscaped, location. Surrounding structures—including an 1869 cabin—as well as a variety of implements were collected here in the 1940s and 1950s. Together they tell a compelling tale.

Before taking the trail, check out the shop and restaurant. (A few dining alternatives are close by on US 58 at Meadows of Dan, a recommended stop.)

Mabry Mill is among the most active interpretive sites on the Parkway. Signs throughout the area explain the exhibits, and during the warmer months this is one of the Parkway's principal living-history sites. The gristmill often operates Friday through Sunday, and interpreters offer talks about the process. Blacksmithing demonstrations occur Wednesday through Sunday, and weaving and spinning take place at various times. Sunday 2:00 to 5:00 p.m., mountain music and dancing bring out the locals.

Edwin Mabry, a miner, blacksmith, and chair maker, built the mill in 1910. He and his wife, Mintoria "Lizzie" Mabry, lived here until 1936, grinding corn for the Meadows of Dan community. In 1945 the National Park Service restored and landscaped the mill. Significant restoration of the structure took place over winter 2002, financed through national park user fees authorized by Congress.

Starting at the mill side of the restaurant/gift shop, pass the no picnicking sign and pause on the left at the paved patio. This is the quintessential view of Mabry Mill.

Head left at the first junction—the prescribed way to go. A short side trail veers left 100 feet beyond and showcases the action of the overshot wheel. Going uphill, take the boardwalk left along one of the many wooden aqueducts that permit this water-hungry mill to work so well. This is one of the auxiliary water sources that feed the main mill-race—a necessity because this mill does not gain sufficient waterpower from its main stream. You'll see the origin of this side source of water, and perhaps gain a better understanding of Mabry's ingenious system, on the way back.

Off the boardwalk, turn left and go through the blacksmith shop and down to the mill. On the way you'll learn that the Mabrys eventually employed an engine to turn the wheel, just before the wide availability of flour from roller mills around the country made gristmills obsolete. Beyond the mill is a display of millstones.

Turn right along the Parkway and you'll next encounter a log cart used to haul timber. Not far beyond is one of the Parkway's neatest cabins—the Matthews Cabin. Built near Galax in 1869, the rustic structure was donated to the Parkway and moved here in 1956 after its metal roofing and outer weatherboarding were removed. In season you can go inside to see cloth being woven on an old loom. The Mabrys built a frame house on this site in 1914—not uncommon at the time due to the prevalence of small sawmills in rural areas. Hikers in the nearby Rocky Knob Recreation Area can see a home from that same era, the Austin House, just 1.5 miles from the lower trailhead on the Rock Castle Gorge Trail.

Past the cabin is a bark mill, a horse-powered machine that ground oak and hemlock bark for tannin used to make bark liquor (a tanning treatment for hides). Not far beyond, look over the edge of the bluff and down on the creekside makings of a different kind of liquor—a moonshine still. An illustration depicts how corn was efficiently turned into a portable, and potable, commodity—corn whiskey.

Corn meal, malt, and sugar were mixed with water and fermented in barrels like the ones you see to the right when you look down. When the fermented mash, called beer, was ready (the process can take two weeks), it was heated in the copper still atop the stone-lined furnace. The vapors would condense in a coil immersed in constantly circling cold water. The liquid then collected in a bucket and was usually run through the still twice to enhance its potency. Up to twenty gallons of corn whiskey could be produced in a night. Water was key to the process in these well-watered mountains. If you look beyond the still, you see the dam that feeds the second of the mill's two flumes.

Continuing, the trail crosses the stream and then makes a right turn. A left leads to the overflow parking area and comfort station opposite the Parkway side of the mill. Just beyond is a sorghum press, another horse-powered squeezing device used to make the sweet substitute for maple syrup that became popular during the Civil War. Continue right; the evaporator where juice from the squeezing process is cooked sits on the left side of the path (one gallon of syrup is made from ten gallons of extract).

Bearing right, pass a horse-drawn wagon and go left, back through the blacksmith's shop. The boardwalk you came in on goes right (the fastest way back to your car). Continue past a variety of plows and farm implements, over the not-so-rushing stream that should be the mill's main water source, and into a forest of white pines to the last leg of the loop. A paved left soon leads in a short distance to VA 603—access to overflow parking on the left by the comfort station and a more remote employee lot to the right.

Just beyond the turnoff is a great view to the left of the impressive wooden aqueduct that feeds the upper end of the

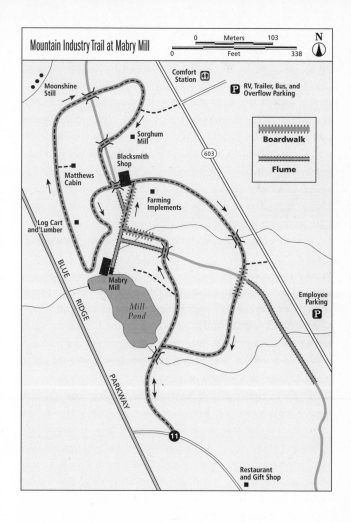

0   Meters   103

0   Feet   338

N

Moonshine
Still

Comfort
Station

P RV, Trailer, Bus, and
Overflow Parking

Sorghum
Mill

Boardwalk

603

Blacksmith
Shop

Flume

Matthews
Cabin

Farming
Implements

Log Cart
and Lumber

Mabry
Mill

Mill
Pond

Employee
Parking

P

BLUE

RIDGE

11

PARKWAY

Restaurant
and Gift Shop

flume at the start of the hike. Off to the left, the neighboring
stream that would otherwise rush into the millpond is raised
up by a wooden aqueduct and carried to where it flows

through the flume beneath you and into the mill's main race. An overflow on the wooden aqueduct permits excess water to spill out. To see how this stream is diverted into the aqueduct, and perhaps more fully understand the ingenuity of Mabry's system, take the paved trail behind you to VA 603 and walk right on the road to where the aqueduct starts behind the restaurant/gift shop.

Returning, the path dips past the leftward view of the aqueduct. As you descend, remnants of the diverted stream flow to the left of the trail and into the pond at the spot where you started your hike. If you walk away with nothing else, an appreciation of Mabry's system aptly illustrates why the Appalachians have long been called the "land of make do."

Key Points

0.1 Reach Mabry Mill.

0.2 Turn left to walk road to start of flume.

0.3 Arrive back at trail and go left on last leg to parking lot.

12 Cumberland Knob Trail and High Piney Spur (Mileposts 217.5 and 218.6)

Enjoy an easy amble to a classic stone picnic shelter atop Cumberland Knob, the spot where Parkway construction started. A nearby wheelchair-accessible path affords a nice view.

Parkway milepost: 217.5–218.6
Distance: Cumberland Knob, loops of 0.4 and 0.7 mile; High Piney Spur, 200 yards out and back
Difficulty: Easy

Elevation gain: 100 feet
Maps: *USGS Cumberland Knob, VA/NC;* parkway map available at www.nps.gov/blri/planyourvisit/brochures.htm

Finding the trailhead: Park near the information/comfort station in the Cumberland Knob Picnic Area. Walk to the right of the building and through the porch to the sign that reads woodland trail.

For the High Piney Spur hike, take the short spur road from Fox Hunter's Paradise Overlook (Milepost 218.6).

The Hikes

Cumberland Knob

Less than a mile south of the Virginia–North Carolina line, an appropriately placed historical marker calls the Parkway "the first rural national parkway." This is Cumberland Knob, the Parkway's first recreation area and the place where construction of the high road started on September 11, 1935. A nice hike loops over this gentle summit.

At the information/comfort station, two paved trails go right from the woodland trail sign. (Please consult the map while reading this narrative to avoid confusion.) The shortest, easiest loop hike to Cumberland Knob goes hard right past a graveyard and up the paved path along the picnic tables near the parking lot. (The more leftward paved path through the meadow is your return route.) As the path leaves the meadow beyond the picnic tables, the paving stops and the trail rises over a rougher treadway. It emerges at the summit on the right side of an old stone-and-log shelter with a shake roof and a fireplace.

Turn left across the front of the shelter—there's not much of a view from the rocks in front—and take the trail back into the woods. This gradual descent swings right to intersect Gully Creek Trail at an unsigned junction. Go left; the path quickly becomes paved as it crosses the meadow to the information station, for a loop of 0.4 mile. (The easiest hike to Cumberland Knob is an out-and-back walk on this return side of this loop.)

A longer walk starts the same way, but just past the shelter turn right at a signed junction where a trail scoots through the rhododendron. The path descends rather steeply to a signed junction with Gully Creek Trail (the first trail to the left you encounter near the end of the Gully Creek Trail). A left at the sign soon passes the unsigned trail junction mentioned above and arrives at the information station for a 0.7-mile hike.

You can reverse either of these routes or omit the trail that rises along the picnic tables and just use the two leftward paths.

Key Points

0.2 Summit shelter.

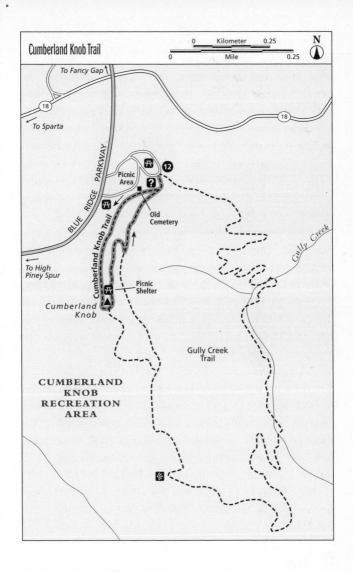

Cumberland Knob Trail

Kilometer 0 — 0.25
Mile 0 — 0.25

N

To Fancy Gap

18

To Sparta

BLUE RIDGE PARKWAY

Picnic Area

12

Old Cemetery

To High Piney Spur

Cumberland Knob Trail

Cumberland Knob

Picnic Shelter

18

Gully Creek

Gully Creek Trail

CUMBERLAND KNOB RECREATION AREA

High Piney Spur

There's an even shorter trail nearby with a striking distant view. Just a mile or so south of Cumberland Knob, at Milepost 218.6, take the spur road from Fox Hunter's Paradise Overlook to a lot at High Piney Spur. A level and paved wheelchair-accessible path leads just 100 yards to a striking viewpoint. It's so short that the sign just says pedestrian walkway.

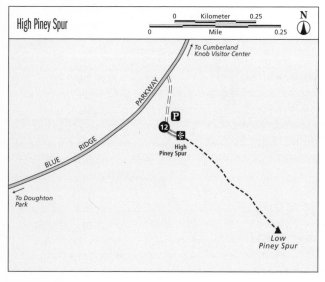

The path leaves a shady bluff that projects away from the Parkway at 2,830 feet and terminates at a stone observation deck on the very prow of High Piney Spur, a dramatically airy perch with a great view into the Piedmont.

13 Wildcat Rocks and Fodder Stack (Milepost 241.1)

The abrupt, spectacular escarpment of Doughton Park plunges 2,000 feet from rocky cliffs into Basin Cove, a remote mountain community now reverting to wilderness. An easy paved trail reaches a view of Caudill Cabin far below, and a rugged but short scramble leads to a spectacular crag—both from the same trailhead.

Parkway milepost: 241.1
Distance: 0.3 mile out and back for Wildcat Rocks; 2.0 miles out and back for Fodder Stack
Difficulty: Easy for Wildcat Rocks; moderate for Fodder Stack

Elevation gain: Negligible
Maps: *USGS Whitehead;* Parkway map available at ranger station (Milepost 245.5) and other park facilities and online at www.nps.gov/blri/planyourvisit/brochures.htm

Finding the trailhead: Turn east off the Parkway to the Doughton Park lodge and picnic area and bear left at the turn to Bluffs Lodge. Park on the right in front of the second lodge unit for the Wildcat Rocks Trail, or continue left into the farther parking lot for Fodder Stack (and a shorter trail to Wildcat Rocks).

The Hikes

Both of these walks start near the lodge on the broad bluff that juts out into the void over Basin Cove, the deep watershed that makes Doughton Park such a scenic stop on the Parkway.

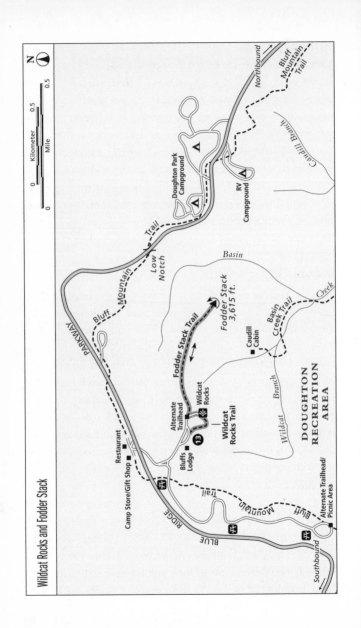

Wildcat Rocks and Fodder Stack

Wildcat Rocks

Wildcat Rocks is the pinnacle beyond the lodge, where a rocky outcrop and stone wall survey the entire 6,000-acre watershed (one of only two places on the Parkway where overnight backpacking is permitted). Peer over, past the summer wildflowers that cling to the rock, and Caudill Cabin sits far below. Start in front of the lodge and take the paved, gently rising path to the rocks and back. (For a shorter stroll, head to the second parking lot near the start of the Fodder Stack Trail, where a bas-relief bust honors Robert Doughton.) Take the ascending paved path up to the right. Some people picnic on the sunny rocks.

Fodder Stack

Nearby Fodder Stack is aptly named—it's a bumpy lump that juts out from the main ridge and stands on its own above steeply dropping terrain. The trail combines great views with moderate walking, and the Park Service recommends the hike to families. The trail veers left off the back of the parking lot and descends steeply on switchbacks to a bench amid great views down to Caudill Cabin. The trail passes a few more benches and a rocky viewpoint on the right as it reaches and follows the ridgeline then ends at a final bench on the summit. In the leafless seasons, the surrounding expanse creates a stunning feeling of being out in the middle of it all.

Despite the seeming wildness of the chasm below, the isolated valley was once a bustling community with a school, store, church, and post office. The first residents moved in after the Civil War, and the last moved out after the flood of 1916. If you'd like a closer look at a pioneer structure similar to Caudill Cabin, head a short distance north to Milepost

238.5 and take the easy path to rustic Brinegar Cabin. This former home of a weaver still contains a loom.

Key Points

0.1 Bench with a view of Caudill Cabin.

0.5 Rocky crag on right with nice view.

1.0 Bench at summit view.

14 Cascades Trail (Milepost 271.9)

One of the Parkway's best interpretive nature trails leads to a wonderful waterfall.

Parkway milepost: 271.9
Distance: 1.0-mile loop
Difficulty: Moderate

Elevation gain: 170 feet
Maps: USGS Maple Springs

Finding the trailhead: Park in the Cascades Parking Area, where the trail goes left at the restroom building. A picnic area surrounds the opposite end of the parking lot, where the Tompkins Knob Trail connects.

The Hike

This trail offers a great sense of the ecological community that teeters on the escarpment of the Blue Ridge. The path wanders the crest of cliffs overlooking the Piedmont and brings hikers to Falls Creek just as a waterfall leaps over the edge. The trail then swings back from the brink along the stream as it tumbles through a quiet valley toward the falls.

Trees are the subject of the trail's twenty interpretive plaques. Between the drier location at cliffside and the well-watered stream drainage, hikers will encounter many of the tree species that populate Blue Ridge forests.

Leaving the parking lot on a paved trail that becomes gravel, go right at the start of the loop to undulate along the crest of the cliff. Winter views are particularly good of an idyllic pastoral scene. You'll marvel at the meadow-covered farming community suspended just below the Blue Ridge and surrounded by the forested slopes of lower mountains. There's a bench on which you can ponder what you'll learn about dogwood, tulip tree, pignut, black locust, serviceberry, mountain laurel, white oak, flame azalea, minniebush, highbush blueberry, and chestnut oak.

The trail dips left into the rhododendron and arcs down to a rustic log bridge across Falls Creek. Across the creek, the return loop trail goes left. Turn right past a dog hobble–describing plaque and quickly descend stone steps to an upper rock wall–encircled observation platform where the stream jumps over the edge and down a steeply sloping slab of rock. The lower platform affords an even better view.

Please stay behind the guardrail. People have fallen to their death at these falls. The falls are best in spring, after a rain, or in winter, when ice holds water in place.

Go right at the return loop junction, with the stream on your left. A treadway nicely underpinned with rock leads to a bridge across the stream. With the stream now on your right, and the Parkway above it obscured in summer by vegetation, pause at one of the two upcoming benches. Birches, rhododendron, sweet birch, witch hazel, eastern hemlock, black gum, and red maple are all species that favor these shady streambanks. The trail turns left and rises to the junction you passed earlier atop the ridge. Head right, back to the parking area. There's evidence of increasing off-trail wandering: Please heed the Park Service sign asking that hikers stay on designated trails.

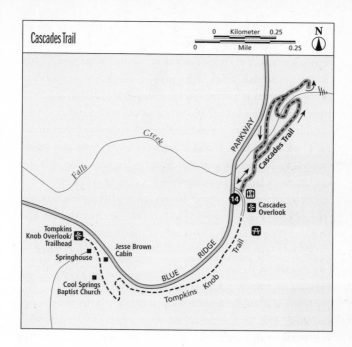

Cascades Trail

Key Points

0.0 Shortly after the start, go right where loop splits.

0.3 Cross log bridge over stream; go right at junction.

0.4 Upper falls view with lower platform 150 feet below.

0.5 Bear right at junction.

0.9 Bear right at final junction to parking lot.

15 Tompkins Knob Trail (Milepost 272.5)

A trail through a wonderful white pine forest inspires appreciation for early mountain structures.

Parkway milepost: 272.5
Distance: 1.2 miles out and back

Difficulty: Easy
Elevation gain: Negligible
Maps: USGS Maple Springs

Finding the trailhead: Park at the Tompkins Knob Parking Area and take an immediate left from your car along the Parkway. The less-than-obvious path dips across the grassy decline into the woods (where it becomes more obvious).

The Hike

This pleasant path offers a choice between a stroll to three interesting historic structures and a longer walk to the picnic area at the nearby parking for the Cascades Trail. You could include the Cascades for an even longer hike.

The shorter stroll is highlighted by intriguing structures from the late nineteenth century—a cabin, adjacent springhouse, and a shelter that served as a rustic church (don't expect a steeple). No elaborate living-history displays take place here, and there's no popular Parkway concession area nearby—just quiet aplenty to imagine life more than a hundred years ago.

Head through the woods along the Parkway and emerge below Jesse Brown's Cabin, a late-nineteenth-century residence moved here to be closer to Cool Spring, the lofty seepage trickling out of the ground in two places to your right beside a tiny decaying springhouse. Head down the short distance to examine this vanishing structure. Water gurgles out of the mossy rocks above the little building with some force. Below that sits a smaller seep that is artfully funneled through the springhouse. The water trickles from the ground along one channeled-out log and into a larger log that directs the flow through the structure. The water's summertime temperature of 40-some degrees no doubt nicely chilled food stored inside the shady, once-weatherized enclave.

The cabin and its impressive fireplace are worth a look, too. Farther up the gradual hill is the "Baptist church" named for Cool Spring—more a shelter used when the weather didn't cooperate when circuit-riding preachers were on hand to minister to high-hollow residents.

Head left at the sign describing the church and descend gently through shady hardwoods past a bench—the greatest elevation change on the whole walk. From here all the way to the Cascades Trail parking and picnic area, it's a largely level saunter under inspiring white pines, where the whisper of the trees mingles with the whoosh of the occasional passing car. That last piney section of trail could be a nice out-and-back stroll from the Cascades Parking Area; the cabins are a nice walk from there too. From either direction, the entire trail is 0.6 mile, with the round-trip a very easy 1.2 miles.

Better yet, ambitious hikers can start from the Tompkins Knob Parking Area and hike to the Cascades, turning the 1.0-mile waterfall walk into a really pleasant 2.4-mile hike.

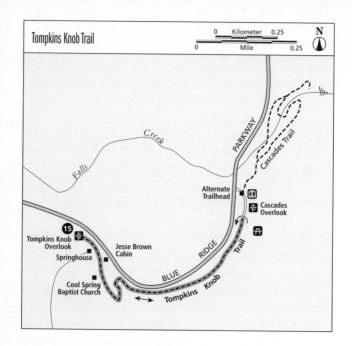

Tompkins Knob Trail

Key Points

0.1 Pass between Jesse Brown's Cabin and springhouse.

0.2 Enter the woods beyond Cool Spring Baptist Church and shortly pass first bench.

0.5 Second bench.

0.6 E. B. Jeffress Park Picnic Area and Cascades Trail parking.

The High Country

Mileposts 276.4 (US 421 at Deep Gap) to
384.7 (US 74 at Asheville)

From Deep Gap at US 421 (Milepost 276.4) to Asheville, North Carolina, at US 74 (Milepost 384.7), the Parkway traverses what can only be called the High Country corner of North Carolina. Ironically, the highest spot on the Parkway is not here—it's south of Asheville.

But everything else about this area says lofty, indeed, almost alpine. At Grandfather Mountain the Blue Ridge escarpment rises to its greatest relief—nearly a vertical mile above the surrounding Piedmont. The computer-designed span of the Linn Cove Viaduct—the Parkway's newest section, completed in 1987—puts you right in the middle of it. Easily accessible just 5 miles off the Parkway is Mount Mitchell (6,684 feet), the East's highest summit. Trails at both locations deserve your attention.

But there are two sides to the High Country. The first half of this Parkway section is bordered by private lands, some of it developed and a popular resort area. The second half is again wrapped in national forest lands. In the High Country you get the Parkway at both ends of a spectrum.

The resort experience is on the northern end—where it's been since the 1880s, when the lowland rich first fled the summer heat to spark tourism in the mountains. They came for the South's coolest summer temperatures and, later, golf at classic, still-popular hostelries like Blowing Rock's Green Park Inn and the classic, chestnut bark–covered luxury of Linville's historic Eseeola Lodge.

The inns and shops of Main Street in the quaint town of Blowing Rock epitomize the appeal of the High Country tourist towns. The town's namesake destination, the Blowing Rock, is a crag with a great view and an Indian legend. It bills itself as "North Carolina's first travel attraction." Early history is the focus at Boone's summer outdoor drama Horn in the West, the inspiring, little-known story of how High Country mountaineers marched over their mountains and down to defeat the British in one of the American Revolution's pivotal battles.

Other area burgs include Linville, at the base of Grandfather Mountain, one of the United States' first planned resort communities. Banner Elk's special license plates call it the ski capital of the south for Beech and Sugar Mountains, the region's southernmost major ski areas. And Boone, the "Hub of the High Country," is a granola-inclined college town, home to Appalachian State University. The village of Valle Crucis claims the 125-year-old Mast General Store, which the late Charles Kuralt called "America's premier country store."

It goes without saying that there are copious craft shops and country clubs here, and the area's diverse dining is as good as or better than that in most of the surrounding cities of the Piedmont.

Parkway facilities in the High Country include Julian Price Memorial Park (Milepost 296.9), a major picnic area and campground memorably sited beside Price Lake. Linville Falls (Milepost 316.4) also has a campground and a large picnic area. Crabtree Meadows (Milepost 339.5) has a campground and snack bar. The summit state park at Mount Mitchell (Milepost 355) also has a restaurant and small tent camp area (highest in the East).

Don't forget camping in the Pisgah National Forest. Nearer to Mount Mitchell are classic campgrounds, such as Black Mountain, nestled in the virgin forest at the base of the mountain. There are a few additional campgrounds far below Grandfather Mountain in a huge dirt road–laced region called Wilson Creek.

Environmental awareness is easy to cultivate on this stretch of the Parkway. The Museum of North Carolina Minerals (Milepost 330.9) is newly renovated and one of the best such exhibits anywhere. Just off the Parkway, Grandfather Mountain's Nature Museum and environmental wildlife habitats are first rate. Mount Mitchell also has a new nature museum and a new wheelchair-accessible summit tower with horizon-identifying plaques. Just a few miles east of the town of Linville Falls on US 221 is Linville Caverns—North Carolina's only commercial cavern.

Museum-quality crafts are also in evidence. Between the Parkway Craft Center in the Manor House at Moses H. Cone Memorial Park (Milepost 294) and the stunning original works of art for sale in the Folk Art Center (Milepost 382), you'll be astonished at the vibrancy of Appalachian handcrafts. The artisans who create these works get their training not far off the Parkway at the world-renowned Penland School of Crafts.

All in all, the High Country may be the high point of the Parkway experience.

16 Figure Eight Trail (Milepost 294.0)

This intriguingly designed trail explores a Northern-type forest that characterizes 3,500-acre Moses H. Cone Memorial Park, one of the Parkway's best places to pause. On this interpretive trail, hikers walk away with a sense of the local woods and Moses Cone (1857–1908), the industrialist whose estate became part of the Parkway.

Parkway milepost: 294.0
Distance: 0.7-mile loop with figure eight
Difficulty: Easy
Elevation gain: Negligible

Maps: *USGS Blowing Rock;* Parkway map available in season at Cone Manor House/Parkway Craft Center and online at www.nps.gov/blri/planyourvisit/brochures.htm

Finding the trailhead: Park at the Cone Manor House/Parkway Craft Center and descend to the manor house. Cross the front porch, descend the front steps, and turn right across the lawn to the trail sign by the woods.

The Hike

This very easy hike should be your first walk in Moses Cone Park. Even if you're not the artsy type, at least briefly explore the craft center in the Manor House (or save it for later), then take in Mr. and Mrs. Cone's favorite path, the one they shared with guests. It gives a real sense of their world—often in the evocative wording of plaques that introduce you to the forest and the culture of the mountaineers who were the couple's neighbors. The plaques "endeavour to interpret for you" the mountaineers' uses for the trees.

The gravel path barely climbs along the edge of the rhododendron and splits. Take the left turn at 0.1 mile through impressive rhododendron reaching for the sky. The trail parallels the road below the house, becomes underpinned on the left by stonework, and then turns right and heads back the way it came.

Halfway back, a right turn at 0.3 mile leads into the namesake figure eight that's hidden within the loop. Like the much larger "Maze" section of carriage road above Bass Lake, this little detour through dense rhododendron is instantly disorienting—and no doubt reflective of what the Cones loved about their densely wooded Blue Ridge estate. Just follow the arrows around, taking a right back on the main path at 0.4 mile.

Impressive hardwoods such as oak, red maple, hickory, and black cherry cluster inside the trail loop. Toward the trail's end, spruce and fir mix in to lend a Northern feel. The flat terrain makes this an excellent cross-country ski trail.

Signs tell how the mountaineers used the trees (tea made from black cherry bark was good for coughs, and the wood "warps not at all") or how a tree was named (serviceberry, "sarvis," bloomed when the circuit rider's church "sarvices" resumed in spring).

By the time you leave the woods behind the massive manor at about 0.7 mile, you're in the perfect frame of mind to pause at one of the final plaques and "visualize the feudal elegance of this elite estate set down in the midst of mountaineer country."

At trail's end you're more than ready to nod at the man who "made his mark the classic American way, by hard work, dedication, and a dream" and left the fruits of his

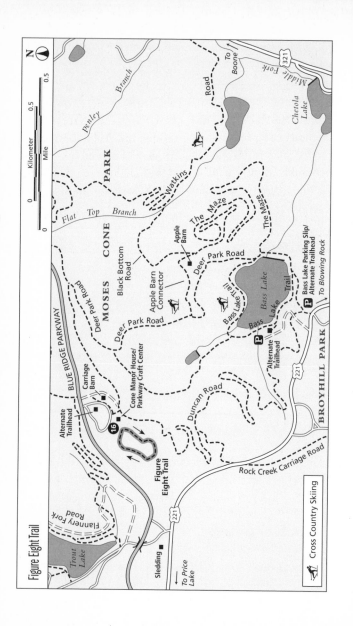

Figure Eight Trail

labors "for all Americans to enjoy." Cone amassed a fortune by popularizing blue denim cloth in the state's post–Civil War textile industry and became known as "The Denim King." He moved to the mountains from Greensboro, North Carolina, at the turn of the twentieth century. With the heart of a preservationist and the mind of a forester, he created lakes in his mountain estate and offered jobs in the new orchards and fields to original landowners still living on the property. This trail nods at what he learned from the locals.

Key Points

0.1 Turn left onto loop.

0.3 Turn right into figure eight.

0.4 Turn right out of figure eight.

0.7 Arrive back at manor house.

17 Bass Lake Loop (Milepost 294.6)

This hike is a circumambulation of Moses Cone Park's prettiest lake.

Parkway milepost: 294.6
Distance: 0.8-mile loop from the lakeshore parking lot; 1.6-mile loop from US 221 trailhead
Difficulty: Easy
Elevation gain: Negligible

Maps: *USGS Blowing Rock;* Parkway map available online at www.nps.gov/blri/planyourvisit/brochures.htm and seasonally at Cone Manor House/Parkway Craft Center

Finding the trailheads: Exit the Parkway at Milepost 294.6 to US 221. Turn left and descend in about a mile to the Bass Lake entrance and its two trailheads. The first is a left turn into a paved road that drops to a parking area on the banks of Bass Lake. Just beyond that turn, also on the left, the roadside Bass Lake parking slip is usable when snow complicates access to the lakeshore parking area.

The Hike

This is an easy, extremely scenic loop that, although unpaved, might be suitable for wheelchairs in dry weather. The Bass Lake loop is easiest from the lakeshore parking area below US 221.

Take a right—or left—out of the lot; there really isn't a preferred direction (this description goes right). The grade weaves in and out along the grassy lakeshore amid maples and reaches a junction right at 0.2 mile—the 0.4-mile side trail to the parking slip on US 221.

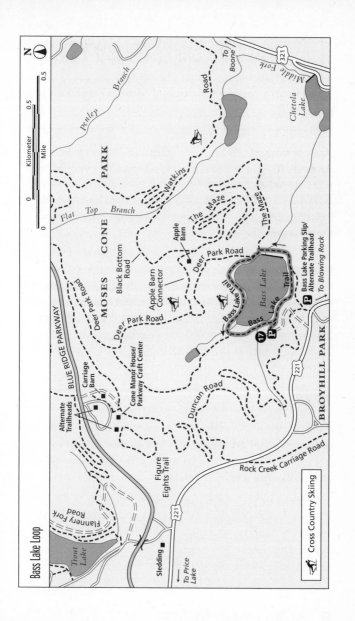

Bass Lake Loop

MOSES CONE PARK

Penley Branch

Flat Top Branch

Watkins Road

To Boone

321

Middle Fork

Chetola Lake

The Maze

The Maze

Apple Barn

Deer Park Road

Black Bottom Road

Apple Barn Connector

Deer Park Road

Deer Park Road

BLUE RIDGE PARKWAY

Carriage Barn

Cone Manor House/ Parkway Craft Center

Alternate Trailheads

Figure Eights Trail

Duncan Road

Bass Lake Trail

Bass Lake

Bass Lake Trail

Bass Lake Trail

P

P

Bass Lake Parking Slip/ Alternate Trailhead

To Blowing Rock

BROYHILL PARK

221

Rock Creek Carriage Road

221

Flannery Fork Road

Trout Lake

Sledding

To Price Lake

N

0   0.5   Kilometer

0   0.5   Mile

Cross Country Skiing

Head left across the dam with the Cone Manor House visible well above the lake. Across the dam, keep left as The Maze trail bears right. Cross a span over the lake's outlet, and then a second road goes right (part of a circuit hike up to the Cone Manor House). In the area where the second carriage road veers right, you may notice the stone base of a boathouse down on the lakeshore at about 0.3 mile.

Continue left around the lake; your parking area is visible beyond an island on the opposite shore. The trail turns right and then left around the upper end of the lake where a bridge crosses the inlet brook at 0.6 mile. There's another bridge soon after, where hikers with dogs step off the trail to give them a drink. From here it's a few hundred feet back to the parking area for an 0.8-mile loop.

Starting at the parking area on US 221, hikers pass an iron gate and gradually descend about 0.1 mile to a T junction with Duncan Road. The access road to the lakeshore parking area is just to the left, and a sign indicates that the Manor House is 2.6 miles in that direction across the access road. (Heading left here across the road takes you on the 4.6-mile circuit hike to the manor that returns to the lake at the spot mentioned above.) Bearing right, reach the lake 0.4 mile from your car. Turn right to cross the dam. The added access distance makes this a 1.6-mile loop.

Key Points from Lakeshore Parking

0.2 Bear left where road goes right to US 221.

0.3 Keep left across dam; avoid two roads to the right.

0.6 Major inlet brook feeds Bass Lake.

0.8 Arrive back at lakeshore parking area.

18 Trout Lake Loop and Rich Mountain Carriage Road (Milepost 294.6)

Unlike popular Bass Lake, with its grassy banks and deciduous trees, Trout Lake—its shores covered in a forest of towering hemlocks—is far less visited. This is also a great starting point for a long and quiet hike higher on Rich Mountain.

Parkway milepost: 294.6
Distance: 1.0-mile lakeshore loop; 2.6-mile circuit of lower Rich Mountain Carriage Road; 6.6-mile circuit to Rich Mountain summit
Difficulty: Easy for lakeshore hike; moderate to more challenging for the longer walks

Elevation gain: Negligible around lake; 610 feet to Rich Mountain
Maps: USGS Blowing Rock; Parkway map available online at www.nps.gov/blri/planyourvisit/brochures.htm and in season at Cone Manor House/Parkway Craft Center

Finding the trailhead: Access the trailhead from Shull's Mill Road, best reached from the US 221–Parkway junction 0.5 mile south of Cone Manor. Exit the Parkway at Milepost 294.6 and turn right onto Shull's Mill Road. Descend under the Parkway tunnel, avoiding the first, abrupt right to the unpaved Flannery Fork Road. Take the second, oblique right immediately past that. The scenic one-way road leads level above the lake to the Trout Lake Parking Area. The exit road returns to Shull's Mill Road at the first trailhead for the Rich Mountain hike (go left 0.5 mile back to the Parkway).

The Hikes

Trout Lake Loop

Trout Lake makes for a memorable lakeshore walk or cross-country ski trip through a nice forest.

From the edge of the Trout Lake Parking Area, take one of the two access trails that dip to the carriage road below; go right. In a short distance take a left onto the road you just drove in on. As you near Shull's Mill Road, turn left and dip down into the woods again. You'll pass a junction at 0.4 mile where the Rich Mountain Carriage Road comes in on the right (the Cone Manor House is 1.0 mile to the right). At 0.5 mile reach Flannery Fork Road; turn left to cross the dam. Some Trout Lake hikers park here on the Flannery Fork Road (a secluded unpaved byway to Boone that's worth the detour).

Across the dam, the trail enters a towering, centuries-old hemlock forest that Cone found in the moist coves that became this lake. (Sadly the hemlock woolly adelgid is killing these centuries-old trees.) There's a junction at 0.7 where the Rich Mountain Carriage Road goes right (more below). Stay left across the bridge to continue through tall trees and glimpses of a northern lakeshore scene. Take either of the two side trails right and uphill to the parking area for a 1.0-mile hike.

Key Points

0.4 Rich Mountain Carriage Road comes in on right.

0.7 Rich Mountain Carriage Road goes right.

1.0 Parking area.

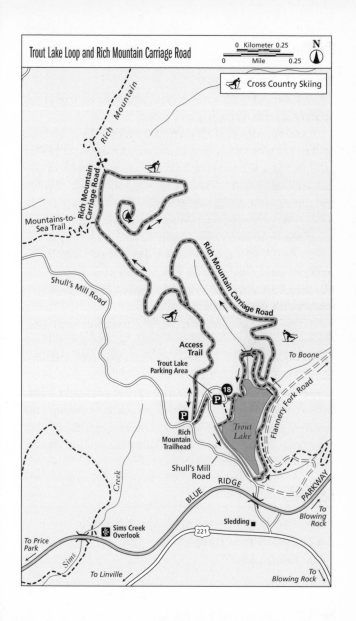

Trout Lake Loop and Rich Mountain Carriage Road

Rich Mountain

0   Kilometer   0.25
0   Mile   0.25

N

Cross Country Skiing

Rich Mountain Carriage Road

Mountains-to-Sea Trail

Shull's Mill Road

Rich Mountain Carriage Road

To Boone

Access Trail

Trout Lake Parking Area

18

P

Flannery Fork Road

Trout Lake

P

Rich Mountain Trailhead

Shull's Mill Road

BLUE RIDGE PARKWAY

To Price Park

Creek

Sims Creek Overlook

221

Sledding

To Blowing Rock

Sims

To Linville

To Blowing Rock

Rich Mountain Carriage Road

The proximity of the trailhead for the Rich Mountain Carriage Road hikes—it's only 100 yards from the Trout Lake parking area—makes this a nice start for more ambitious hikers.

To make a loop of the lake and lower Rich Mountain Carriage Road, take a left from the parking area and enjoy the lakeshore forest for 0.3 mile on the way to a left at the first junction with the Rich Mountain Carriage Road. The trail makes a switchback past a scenic water impoundment with a splashing spillway, then passes through a gate at 1.6 miles. The trail soon exits the woods and at 1.9 miles enters the meadow and reaches a junction just above the main Rich Mountain trailhead on Shull's Mill Road. To the right, the Rich Mountain Carriage Road goes across the meadow to the summit. Turn left and descend the carriage road access trail to Shull's Mill Road at 2.5 miles. At Shull's Mill Road, step across the exit road for the Trout Lake parking area and go left on the gravel road down to the lakeside parking area for a 2.6-mile hike.

You could also go right at the meadow above the trailhead at Shull's Mill Road and reach the summit of Rich Mountain at 3.9 miles. Retrace your steps from there to the top of the carriage road access trail at 5.9 miles, then turn right down to Shull's Mill Road. A left there down to the Trout Lake Parking Area on the gravel road mentioned above makes a 6.6-mile circuit.

19 Price Lake Trail (Milepost 297.2)

A great lakeside loop circles the Parkway's largest body of water.

Parkway milepost: 297.2
Distance: 2.5-mile loop
Difficulty: Easy to moderate
Elevation gain: Negligible

Maps: *USGS Boone;* Parkway map available online at www .nps.gov/blri/planyourvisit/ brochures.htm and in season at campground contact kiosk

Finding the trailhead: Either of two lakeshore overlooks is a potential starting point. The Boone Fork Overlook (oddly named because it overlooks Price Lake) is reached by a spur road at Milepost 297.2. Price Lake Overlook (which also overlooks the lake) is at Milepost 296.7. The route described here starts at the Boone Fork Overlook.

The Hike

Price Lake is a memorable walk, in part through the lakeshore Loop A of Price Lake Campground—easily one of the premier places on the Parkway to set up a tent.

Leaving the southern end of the Boone Fork Overlook by the trail map sign, descend a wheelchair-accessible ramp past the top of the boat launch and behind the boat rental building. The first 0.7 mile of this trail has a number of benches and is wheelchair accessible to stream and lakeshore fishing spots. The trail scoots into the rhododendron immediately and crosses a bridge over Cold Prong. Most of this hike is right on the lakeshore, but the path wanders a bit away and crosses a second bridge over the lake's main source, Boone Fork.

Staying away from the shore, the trail crosses a boggy area on a long boardwalk at about 0.5 mile. Here, opposite the boat launch, the trail returns to the shore at a lakeside fishing deck. This 1.4-mile out-and-back hike is one of the Parkway's best for the wheelchair-bound and beginning or very young cross-country skiers or hikers. From here to the Parkway the trail is a woodsy and quiet walk—excepting the hollow thunk of paddle on canoe—around the longest arm of the lake.

The trail turns right and climbs a very brief uphill through a rhododendron grove before descending back to the lakeshore. The view is of the opposite bank as this prong of the lake constricts to another feeder stream where beaver activity often creates muddy conditions. The trail turns left and crosses a small bridge at about 1.0 mile then bears left again along the opposite bank, bound for the Parkway and the dam that impounds the lake. Just after a small bridge there's a bench tucked down by the lakeshore and surrounded by rhododendron at 1.2 miles. The views of Grandfather Mountain are particularly good along this side of the lake. A variety of rocks reach into the water, enticing boaters to land and fishers to cast.

The trail exits the rhododendron near the bank to turn sharply right around a large rock at 1.4 miles. The path undulates its way to a flight of steps that lead out of the woods to the Parkway at 1.7 miles. Head left across the dam, pass through Price Lake Overlook, and hug the roadside on a paved path. A lakeside deck creates another wheelchair-accessible place to fish or catch a view before leaving the open roadside and entering the tall hemlocks of the campground. The trail follows the lake and then veers right to bisect Loop A. Just past a restroom at 2.2 miles, the

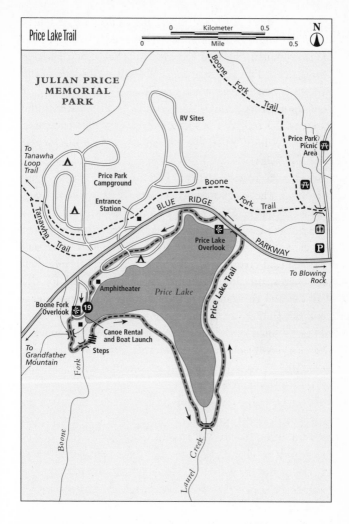

Kilometer
0   0.5

Mile
0   0.5

N

JULIAN PRICE
MEMORIAL
PARK

RV Sites

Price Park
Picnic
Area

To Tanawha
Loop
Trail

Price Park
Campground

Boone

BLUE RIDGE

Fork Trail

Entrance
Station

Tanawha

Trail

Price Lake
Overlook

PARKWAY

To Blowing
Rock

Amphitheater

Price Lake

Price Lake Trail

Boone Fork
Overlook

19

Canoe Rental
and Boat Launch

To
Grandfather
Mountain

Boone

Steps

Fork

Laurel Creek

trail crosses the road into the woods. At a junction go left;
the trail to the right crosses the Parkway to the other campground loops and the Tanawha Trail Parking Area. The

Price Lake Trail rises left to skirt the campground amphi-theater. Emerging at the northern end of the Boone Fork Overlook, follow the edge of the parking lot along the lake and back to your car at 2.5 miles.

Key Points

0.5 Cross lengthy boardwalk.

0.7 Fishing deck opposite boat ramp.

1.0 Bridge signals left turn along final side of the lake.

1.7 Turn left along Parkway to cross dam.

2.2 Pass restrooms.

2.5 Back to Boone Fork Overlook.

20 Tanawha Trail Hikes near Holloway Mountain Road (Milepost 298.6)

Two opportunities—a circuit hike and an out-and-back walk—sample the Tanawha and Mountains-to-Sea Trails in an area noted for outstanding meadow views.

Parkway milepost: 298.6
Distance: 2.4 miles for the circuit to the east of the road; 1.6 miles for the out-and-back hike to the west
Difficulty: Easy for the meadow hikes immediately east and west of Holloway Mountain Road
Elevation gain: 50 feet

Maps: *USGS Grandfather Mountain;* Parkway map available online at www.nps.gov/blri/planyourvisit/brochures.htm and in season at Linn Cove Information Station/Visitor Center (Map does not show the hike described first below; rely on the map provided here)

Finding the trailhead: Leave the Parkway south of Blowing Rock at Milepost 298.6–the Holloway Mountain Road–US 221 exit. Turn immediately right onto the dirt road and park on the right in 1 mile at the Tanawha Trail crossing.

The Hikes

Eastern Circuit

The circuit hike to the east patches together an easy sampling of the Tanawha, Boone Fork, and Mountains-to-Sea Trails without requiring you to completely retrace your steps. It also takes hikers along one of the premier unpaved roads near the Parkway. If you continue 1.2 miles past the trailhead and then turn right onto a paved road, you soon reach NC 105 between Boone and Banner Elk, which makes this the perfect back way into the High Country.

Head through the fat-man squeeze going north (to the right coming from the Parkway) on the combined Tanawha/Mountains-to-Sea Trail. Cross the first stretch of meadow, pass through another squeeze at 0.1 mile, and then turn right onto an old gravel farm road. Follow the grade a short distance beneath a power line at 0.3 mile; at 0.4 mile veer left up the log steps as the trail leaves the grade. At 0.5 mile cross the next fence and pass a Tanawha Trail signpost just beyond it onto another obvious gravel road grade.

Two hundred feet beyond the sign, at about 0.6 mile, the trail goes right on the main grade near the edge of a meadow. Leave the formal trail here, veering uphill where the road grade rises left. Emerge into the meadow and follow the obvious but faint, now-grassy old roadway left for 100 feet parallel to rhododendron at the edge of the woods. It wanders across the meadow, under the power line in the distance, and to the right of the rise beyond.

At about 0.9 mile the grade reaches a junction where the Boone Fork Trail comes in on the left. The junction is marked by a Mountains-to-Sea Trail signpost and signs in two directions reading BOONE FORK TRAIL, 4.9-MILE LOOP. Keep straight; the Boone Fork Trail turns left at the sign and onto your road grade.

Follow the rhododendron-arched Boone Fork Trail straight ahead, or turn right at the sign on an obvious secondary path and go up over the grassy bulge of the meadow for a great view of Grandfather Mountain. Continuing over this meadow, head off the steeper side of the peak and down to the Boone Fork Trail, visible below as it leaves the rho-dodendron tunnel you avoided and arcs to the right across the field below.

Returning to the main trail, descend from the meadow into white pines to a junction at 1.3 miles. This is the Mountains-to-Sea/Tanawha Trail combination that you started on but left back at the meadow. Turn right off the Boone Fork Trail and head south along this section of trail you missed.

The first few hundred yards are beautiful—ferns, moss, and pine needles cover the ground under a grove of white pines. Notice the forgotten ruin of a tiny chestnut farm structure on the left as you start down from the turn. The path crosses a bridge, meets a fenceline, follows it, crosses another small bridge, and gradually climbs right to reenter the meadow at an old apple orchard. Leveling off, the trail switchbacks left and passes a grove of white pines flanked by another apple orchard—a long-ago mountaineer home-site. The trail swings past the site and enters the woods at a trailside pit where an underground stream threatens to collapse the path.

Heading back into the woods at 1.8 miles, you immediately pass the uphill grade you earlier took to the left to exit the formal trail (now on your right). Now you're head-ing back the way you came. If you miss the last left turn from the road grade onto the Tanawha Trail to your car, don't sweat it. The gravel roadway empties onto Holloway Mountain Road 200 feet beyond where you parked (turn left), for a total hike of about 2.4 miles.

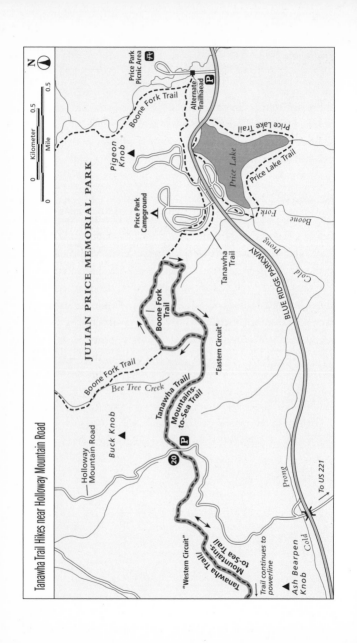

Tanawha Trail Hikes near Holloway Mountain Road

Key Points

0.4 Veer left off the grade and up log steps.

0.9 Join Boone Fork/Mountains-to-Sea Trail.

1.3 Turn right onto Mountains-to-Sea/Tanawha Trail.

1.8 Rejoin portion of trail you've already walked.

2.4 Holloway Mountain Road.

Western Circuit

Just across Holloway Mountain Road from the hike above lies an even easier meadow walk to the west and south. The Tanawha Trail heads toward Grandfather Mountain, and views of the peak dominate the horizon in that direction.

The trail leaves the road through the fat-man squeeze, turns left at the roadside Tanawha Trail mileage sign, and arcs up the edge of the meadow. The path crosses another fence at 0.4 mile below an old cemetery that is just out of sight on the high right. The trail swings into the bowl of the next meadow and then wanders through a grove of white pines with views down on Holloway Mountain Road.

When you reach a power line toward the end of the meadow at about 0.8 mile, a return from there creates an easy, meadow-filled stroll of 1.6 miles that's perfect for a picnic or cross-country ski tour.

21 Tanawha Trail to Rough Ridge (Milepost 302.8)

Quite possibly the Parkway's easiest path to a spectacular view, here the Tanawha Trail traverses the alpine–appearing crest of a leading ridge to Grandfather Mountain.

Parkway milepost: 302.8
Distance: Entire section is 1.5 miles, but the closest view is only a 0.6-mile round-trip. Out-and-back hikes of 1.2 and about 2.0 miles lead to the peak of Rough Ridge.
Difficulty: Easy to moderate
Elevation gain: 540 feet from Wilson Creek Parking Area; 480 feet from Rough Ridge Parking Area

Maps: USGS Grandfather Mountain; Parkway map available online at www.nps.gov/blri/planyourvisit/brochures.htm and in season at Linn Cove Visitor Center. The Grandfather Mountain hiking map shows the trail best and is available free at Grandfather Mountain entrance (south from Rough Ridge Overlook 2.3 miles to US 221 exit; right 1 mile to entrance).

Finding the trailhead: Park at either Wilson Creek Overlook (Milepost 303.6) or Rough Ridge Overlook (Milepost 302.8).

The Hike

The cliff-lined alpine crest of Rough Ridge offers startling vistas atop a stone face visible to Parkway motorists. From many places on this part of the Tanawha Trail, including boardwalks just 0.3 mile from the Rough Ridge Parking Area, the vista engulfs you.

As you're standing on the boardwalks, Rough Ridge rises to the three loftiest summits of Grandfather Mountain—a rocky, dramatic climax at nearly 6,000 feet. The Wilson Creek drainage drops like an expansive chute past the Linn Cove Viaduct and Parkway snaking to the south. Far below, across the rippling corduroy of Pisgah National Forest, the land descends to the edge of the Piedmont. This nearly vertical-mile relief is the greatest rise of the Blue Ridge escarpment. Mount Mitchell lies on the southern horizon; Grandfather Mountain's Pilot Knob is the rocky peak just to the north.

Standing here, it's no wonder that the Tanawha Trail—the Cherokee word means "great hawk" or "eagle"—is the crowning achievement of the Blue Ridge Parkway trail network. The federal government spent almost $750,000 on the 13.5 miles of trail between Beacon Heights, near Linville, and Price Park Campground, near Blowing Rock. Hikers won't fail to notice the trail's intricate stone stairways, rock-paved treadways, and arching wood bridges (lowered here by helicopter). Like the building of the computer-designed span in the distance, the Linn Cove Viaduct, all of these efforts were made to minimize hiker damage to this scenic environment. This is the Grandfather Mountain "missing link" portion of the Parkway—the long-unfinished stretch of the road that opened on September 11, 1987.

From Rough Ridge

Rough Ridge is a scenic high point of this part of the Parkway, and the most direct route to the summit is from the parking area of the same name. Here the access trail ascends log steps to a junction. Take the Tanawha Trail left and immediately cross an arching wood bridge (near a no pets beyond this point sign). Beneath the bridge a cascade tumbles down and directly under the parking area.

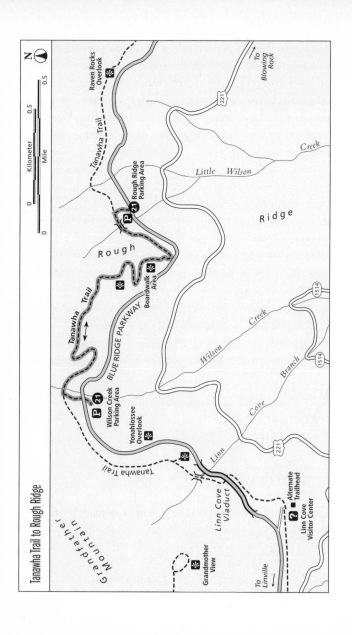

Tanawha Trail to Rough Ridge

N

Grandfather Mountain

Tanawha Trail

Tanawha Trail

Tanawha Trail

Rough

Ridge

Raven Rocks Overlook

Rough Ridge Parking Area

P 21

Little Wilson

Creek

To Blowing Rock

221

Boardwalk Area

BLUE RIDGE PARKWAY

Wilson Creek Parking Area

P 21

Yonahlossee Overlook

Wilson

Creek

Cove

Branch

1514

1514

Linn

221

Linn Cove Viaduct

Grandmother View

Alternate Trailhead

Linn Cove Visitor Center

?

To Linville

0   0.5   Kilometer
0   0.5   Mile

Across the bridge, the often-soggy trail ascends through evergreens, climbs a flight of stone steps, and then levels across a rocky shelf amid blueberry bushes and galax. The trail turns a corner, passes a distinctive stack rock formation on the right, and reaches 200 feet of ascending boardwalk designed to keep hikers from trampling the low vegetation that now surrounds you.

From this boardwalk—just 0.3 mile round-trip from the parking area—the view is remarkably similar to that found on the summit (another 0.3 mile ahead up rocky but nicely graded switchbacks). At the top, cable-defined pathways keep people on the paths amid fragile Allegheny sand myrtle and turkey beard. Unfortunately, dogs that are allowed off-leash don't stay within the barriers, so the Park Service prohibits all dogs on this trail.

Either location is a nice spot to watch a sunset and get back to your car quickly. On a crystal-clear fall day, with electric foliage below, a summit dusting of snow and racing clouds . . . you get the picture.

Key Points

0.3 Boardwalk views.
0.6 Views from the summit of Rough Ridge.

From Wilson Creek Overlook

Wilson Creek Overlook is also a good start for an out-and-back hike to Rough Ridge. This approach is often less populated than the trail from Rough Ridge Parking Area.

Starting at Wilson Creek, take the side trail under the Parkway 0.1 mile to a junction with the Tanawha Trail and go right. Cross Wilson Creek (hence the name of the entire watershed above and below the mountain). The trail drops to within sight of the road and then slips below the prow of an outcrop at 0.2 mile. Then comes a largely gradual and meandering climb across an ecosystem that recommends this Tanawha Trail hike—rock-garden boulder fields strewn with spring wildflowers and towering trees. After climbing through mixed evergreens to a saddle, stone steps artfully surmount the crag-capped summit of Rough Ridge, just under 1.0 mile from the Wilson Creek Parking Area (about 2.0 miles round-trip). From the summit to the Rough Ridge Parking Area, it's another 0.6 mile, for a slightly less than 1.5-mile total hike.

An end-to-end hike would require leaving a car at both parking areas. If that's not possible, consider walking between the trailheads. The roadside walk is only 0.8 mile, and it's recommended by spectacular views that motorists often only glimpse as they whiz by. That makes for a 2.4-mile hike.

22 Linn Cove Viaduct (Milepost 304.4)

A wheelchair-accessible paved path leads under the stunning span of the Parkway's Linn Cove Viaduct and then continues as a rougher trail through beautiful Linn Cove. The turnaround point is a classic postcard view of the viaduct.

Parkway milepost: 304.4
Distance: 0.3 mile out and back for barrier-free trail; 1.0 mile out and back to best view
Difficulty: Easy and barrier-free to moderate
Elevation gain: Virtually none for the paved trail; 50 feet for the moderate hike
Maps: *USGS Grandfather Moun-* *tain;* Parkway handout map, available online at www.nps.gov/ blri/planyourvisit/brochures.htm and in season at Linn Cove Visitor Center. Grandfather Mountain hiking map shows the trail best and is available free at Grandfather Mountain entrance (south 0.7 to US 221 exit; right 1 mile to entrance).

Finding the trailhead: The trail starts at the end of the Linn Cove Parking Area, opposite the small visitor center.

The Hike

The easiest walk to a view of the Linn Cove Viaduct begins at the Linn Cove Visitor Center, just north of Milepost 304. A paved and barrier-free trail winds nearly 0.2 mile from the end of the parking lot opposite the station to a viewpoint underneath the serpentine Linn Cove Viaduct.

The next-easiest walk lies just beyond. Stay on the trail past the pavement as it briefly climbs to the level of the bridge and zigzags through towering rhododendron, hemlocks, and birches. The trail undulates over impressive stone

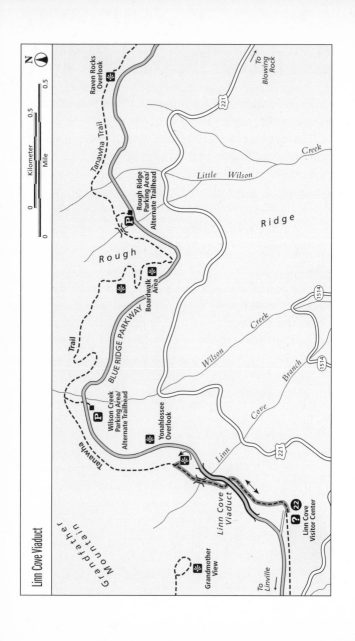

stairways among the jumble of huge boulders that tumble down from Grandfather Mountain's Black Rock Cliffs. This is the terrain that prompted the choice of span you see arcing around you. As you hike, you'll hear the occasional whoosh and thump of a passing car.

The trail crosses a bridge over Linn Cove Branch and ascends out of the stream drainage to a ridgeline above the road. At the 0.5-mile mark take a right on a side trail (a TANAWHA TRAIL sign with arrows that directs hikers back to the Linn Cove Parking Area marks the spot). This rock offers the picture-perfect, oft-photographed view back to the bridge. Retrace your steps for a 1.0-mile round-trip.

Key Points

0.2   End of paved path.
0.5   View of viaduct.

23 Beacon Heights Trail (Milepost 305.2)

A short and popular leg-stretcher affords spectacular views of Grandfather Mountain and its nearly vertical-mile drop to the Piedmont.

Parkway milepost: 305.2
Distance: 0.7 mile out and back
Difficulty: Easy
Elevation gain: About 120 feet
Maps: USGS Grandfather Mountain; Parkway map available online at www.nps.gov/blri/planyourvisit/brochures.htm and in season at Linn Cove Visitor Center. Grandfather Mountain hiking map shows the trail best and is available free at Grandfather Mountain entrance (north 0.1 mile to US 221 exit; right 1 mile to entrance).

Finding the trailhead: The Parkway trailhead is located at Milepost 305.2, 0.1 mile south of the US 221 entrance to the Parkway, 3 miles east of Linville.

The Hike

This is one of the Parkway's best leg-stretchers. The grades are gradual, the footing isn't very difficult, and the views are outstanding.

From the trailhead—at 4,220 feet—walk across a state road that parallels the Parkway (NC 1513) and enter the woods where the sign says TANAWHA TRAIL BEACON HEIGHTS 0.2. The path climbs gradually to a junction. Where the Tanawha Trail starts to the left, turn right onto the Mountains-to-Sea Trail—that's also the Beacon Heights Trail to

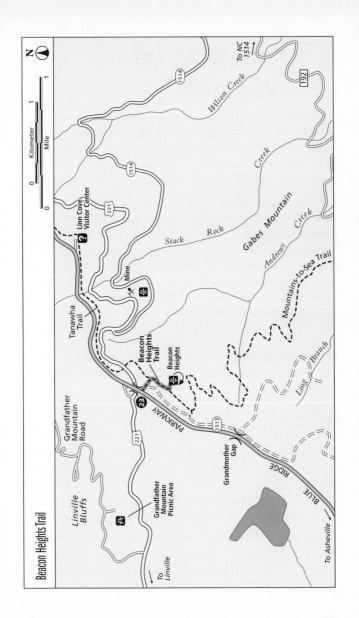

Beacon Heights Trail

the top. You'll pass an overhanging rock on the left that makes an excellent rain shelter. There's a bench on the right before the steepest, rockiest part of the trail.

At a signed junction at 0.2 mile, the Mountains-to-Sea Trail goes right where the Beacon Heights Trail switchbacks left. At about 0.3 mile the Beacon Heights Trail reaches the crest, a bench, and a junction.

To the right, the path emerges on top of a south-facing exfoliated dome with great views to the Piedmont and the high peaks south along the Parkway, including Mount Mitchell and the Linville Gorge. To the left, the path ascends stone steps to spectacular views of the eastern flank of Grandfather Mountain, the Parkway north toward Blowing Rock, and the rippled, waterfall-filled Pisgah National Forest to the east. Retrace your steps to the bottom.

Key Points

0.0 Shortly after starting out, go right on the Mountains-to-Sea Trail where Tanawha Trail goes left.

0.2 Go left. Mountains-to-Sea Trail goes right.

0.3 Reach crest. In another 250 feet, enjoy summit views.

0.7 Arrive back at parking area.

24 Flat Rock Self-Guiding Loop Trail (Milepost 308.3)

This educational trail has good distant views of noteworthy nearby summits.

Parkway milepost: 308.3
Distance: 0.7-mile loop
Difficulty: Moderate

Elevation gain: About 100 feet
Maps: USGS *Grandfather Mountain;* no Parkway map

Finding the trailhead: The trail begins at Milepost 308.3, 0.4 mile south of NC 1511. This local road leads west to Linville and US 221 and east as a gravel road into the Pisgah National Forest.

The Hike

Here's a rare hike—one not to miss for serious hikers and more casual Parkway motorists alike. This is a quick walk to a good view or a wonderful hour-plus stroll for a family that could include nature study or a picnic. This well-maintained, popular trail ascends gradually and then wanders northward along an outcrop with wonderful westward-facing views and a Northern hardwood forest at an elevation of 4,000 feet.

Not far above the parking area, the trail loop splits. Head left at the first interpretive sign bearing David Brower's sage observation that humankind cannot make wilderness, it "can only spare it."

Beyond that junction, just as the trail jogs right, look off in the woods to the left. Parents might ask a child why that tree's standing on its tiptoes. The answer—the yellow

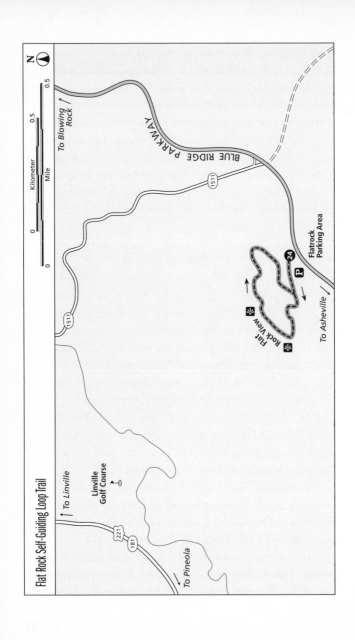

Flat Rock Self-Guiding Loop Trail

birch perched above the forest floor on three foot-long, leglike roots sprouted long ago atop a huge fallen tree called a nursery log and took root around it. When the log rotted away, the birch was left standing on stilts.

Interpretive signs point out a virgin remnant of a northern red oak on the right and then an American chestnut, among others. Then comes withe-rod (Viburnum cassinoides), brewed as a tonic for fever, the sign says, by mountaineers who called it "Shonny Haw." Nearby on Beech Mountain, the East's highest ski area, withe-rod grows at nearly 5,500 feet, where it inspires the same name, but a different spelling, for ski runs Upper and Lower "Shawneehaw."

Next step out onto Flat Rock, a massive crop of quartzite with ribbons of white quartz. The first 50 feet or so makes a wonderful transition from rhododendron woods to a crag with gnarled pines, hemlocks, and luxuriant moss and lichen. These pioneer plant communities struggle to turn the rock into soil and part of the process is Flat Rock's "bathtubs," the interesting bowl-size basins just ahead. The water they usually contain permits windblown waves and freezing and thawing to break down this solid shelf of rock.

Turn right at the cement rectangle with a yellow painted arrow—three of these markers will guide you across a cliff-top that could be an enigma in dense fog, not a rarity here. But on a clear day, the views are extensive.

As you head right along the outcrop, look west across the valley at the distant peaks on a dramatic ridge of summits covered with natural meadows. The Appalachian Trail crosses these alpine-appearing areas called "balds."

Pause where you can see the entire western horizon and notice Yellow Mountain, a Nature Conservancy-owned tract on the leftward end of the ridge. Just to the left of that, a spur of Roan Mountain is visible—noted for its stunning bloom of rhododendron in late June. The prominent grassy peak on the far right end of the ridge is Hump Mountain.

Follow the yellow arrows across the crest to one of the Parkway's best views of Grandfather Mountain.

Reenter the woods that rise in the lee of the rocks; the trail dips gently past a sign that points out both local species of rhododendron growing side by side. The smaller leafed Catawba (Rhododendron catawbiense) blooms reddish purple in early June; the longer leafed rosebay, or great laurel (Rhododendron maximum), blooms white in July.

Where the trail turns right toward the end of the loop, a large bulge on a tree is a burl, a tree cancer the mountaineers used to make bowls (the nearby Grandfather Mountain Nature Museum has a stunningly huge example). At the trail junction, head left back to the parking lot.

Key Points

0.1 Shortly after the start, the trail splits—head left.

0.2 Trail heads onto rocky outcrop.

0.4 Trail leaves outcrop.

0.6 Trail intersects—turn left.

0.7 Arrive back at parking area.

25 Duggers Creek Loop, Linville Gorge Trail, and Plunge Basin Overlook Trail (Milepost 316.4)

Three trails on the visitor center side of the river make the most scenic, least visited hike to Linville Falls.

Parkway milepost: 316.4
Distance: 0.25 mile one way for Duggers Creek Trail; 0.7-mile out and back to Plunge Basin Overlook Trail; 1.4 miles out and back to Linville Gorge (2.0 miles for a combination of the two).
Difficulty: Easy for Duggers Creek Trail; moderate for Plunge Basin Overlook Trail; moderate to more challenging for Linville Gorge Trail
Maps: *USGS Linville Falls;* Parkway map available at trailhead visitor center and campground and online at www.nps.gov/blri/planyourvisit/brochures.htm

Finding the trailhead: The trails to Linville Falls start at a visitor center and parking area 1.5 miles from the Parkway, past the Linville Falls Campground. The spur road to the trailhead leaves the Blue Ridge Parkway between Mileposts 316 and 317, about 1 mile north of the US 221–Blue Ridge Parkway junction at the town of Linville Falls.

In winter, when the Parkway and the Linville Falls Spur Road to the falls can be closed due to snow, an alternative Forest Service trailhead provides access for winter hikers and cross-country skiers. From the US 221–Parkway junction near the town of Linville Falls (1 mile south of where the Linville Falls Spur Road joins the Parkway), go south on US 221 to the community of Linville Falls and turn left onto NC 183. In 0.7 mile from the US 221–NC 183 junction in Linville Falls, turn right onto Wiseman's View Road (NC 1238, also called the Kistler Memorial Highway), where prominent signs direct hikers to Linville Gorge. The Linville Falls trailhead is just a few hundred yards from NC 183 on the left.

The Hikes

Three trails on the visitor center side of the river, two of which make a nice 2.0-mile hike when combined, but a scenic stroll is also possible. All start at about 3,200 feet.

The Duggers Creek Trail links the visitor center with the far end of the recreation area's long parking lot—a 0.2-mile walk you could enjoy heading back to your car after hitting the visitor center. Pass through the visitor center portico by the restrooms and ascend to take a left on Duggers Creek Trail at the junction where the Linville Gorge Trail goes right. The path wanders along beautiful Duggers Creek past plaques with inspiring sayings.

The Linville Gorge Trail heads right at that first junction and ascends gradually through inspiring hemlocks and rhododendron. At 0.3 mile from the visitor center, the Plunge Basin Overlook Trail heads right for the best view of the falls at 0.4 mile. The path is level to a bench, but then turns right and descends at times steeply but briefly down stone steps to a rock-walled perch above the falls. It's a truly inspiring sight. From here it's a 0.7 mile round-trip back to the visitor center.

Back at the junction, the Linville Gorge Trail bears right (a left if you avoid the Plunge Basin View) and reaches a fenced off crag at a height of land before dipping over the edge and down. The gradual path has handrails as it skirts steep drops and then descends a steep flight of steps. Use care at the bottom of the steps—the trail turns hard right, but you could keep going left on the path created by countless others who

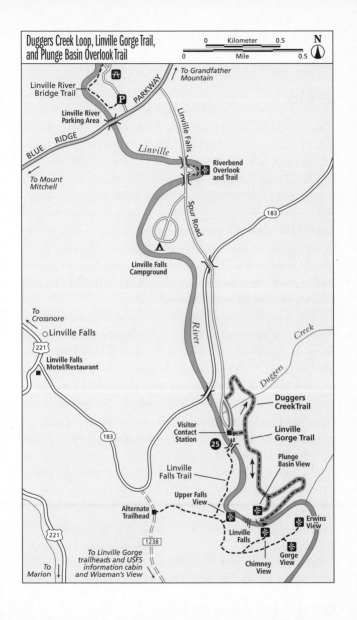

Duggers Creek Loop, Linville Gorge Trail, and Plunge Basin Overlook Trail

Kilometer 0   0.5

Mile 0   0.5

N

Linville River Bridge Trail

Linville River Parking Area

PARKWAY

To Grandfather Mountain

BLUE RIDGE

Linville

To Mount Mitchell

Linville Falls

Riverbend Overlook and Trail

Spur Road

183

Linville Falls Campground

To Crossnore

Linville Falls

221

Linville Falls Motel/Restaurant

River

Duggers Creek

Duggers Creek Trail

183

Visitor Contact Station

25

Linville Gorge Trail

Plunge Basin View

Linville Falls Trail

Upper Falls View

Alternate Trailhead

1238

To Linville Gorge trailheads and USFS information cabin and Wiseman's View

221

Linville Falls

Chimney View

Erwins View

Gorge View

To Marion

have missed the turn. The trail continues a rocky though gradual descent to the bottom of a towering cliff.

The trail descends with river noise off to the left. Avoid the first path left to the water, keeping right to emerge at the water's edge. Rock-hop to a vantage point near the base of the thundering falls (ice may inhibit this in winter). This is a wonderful place to enjoy a lingering lunch at the lowest point of the trail system—about 3,040 feet—and soak up the wild atmosphere of the rock-hewn amphitheater below the falls. The craggy walls mark the start of Linville Gorge. On a warm summer day, the deep expanse of emerald water below the falls will surely tempt you—but swimming isn't allowed.

On a quiet day, amid the wildness and river noise, it's easy to imagine the hemmed-in feeling William Linville and his son must have felt near here in 1766 when confronted by Native Americans—who then scalped them. It's also easy to be grateful to John D. Rockefeller, who donated the virgin-forested parcel to the National Park Service in 1952. Like the Linville Gorge Wilderness itself, this area surrounding the falls has never been logged and contains an inspiring forest. Towering hemlocks and white pines soar above an understory of rhododendron that blooms profusely in late May.

A hike to the base of the falls and back is 1.4 miles. Include the side trip to the Plunge Basin Overlook and it's a 2.0 miler.

Key Points

0.3 Plunge Basin Overlook Trail branches from Linville Gorge Trail.

0.7 Linville Gorge Trail reaches base of falls.

1.4 Arrive back at parking area.

26 Linville Falls Trail (Milepost 316.4)

A variety of options explore virgin forest and rugged scenery near Linville Falls, an impressive cataract that plunges into the Linville Gorge Wilderness. A detour to the short, inspiring Wiseman's View Trail is recommended from the alternative trailhead.

Parkway milepost: 316.4
Distance: 1.0 to 2.0 miles out and back
Difficulty: Easy for Upper Falls View and Wiseman's View; moderate for Chimney, Gorge, and Erwins Views

Maps: *USGS Linville Falls;* Parkway map available at visitor center and campground and online at www.nps.gov/blri/planyour visit/brochures.htm

Finding the trailhead: The trails to Linville Falls start at a visitor center and parking area 1.5 miles from the Parkway, past the Linville Falls Campground. The spur road to the trailhead leaves the Blue Ridge Parkway between Mileposts 316 and 317, about 1 mile north of the US 221–Blue Ridge Parkway junction at the town of Linville Falls.

In winter, when the Parkway and the Linville Falls Spur Road to the falls can be closed due to snow, an alternative Forest Service trailhead provides access for winter hikers and cross-country skiers— and also permits a side trip to the Wiseman's View Trail. From the US 221–Parkway junction near the town of Linville Falls (1 mile south of where the Linville Falls Spur Road joins the Parkway), go south on US 221 to the community of Linville Falls and turn left onto NC 183. In 0.7 mile from the US 221–NC 183 junction in Linville Falls, turn right onto Wiseman's View Road (NC 1238, also called the Kistler Memorial Highway), where prominent signs direct hikers to Linville Gorge. The Linville Falls trailhead is just a few hundred yards from

NC 183 on the left. From there a national forest contact station is 0.5 mile beyond on the right; trailhead parking for Wiseman's View is 3.8 miles on the left.

The Hike

Across the river from the visitor center, nice hikes reach higher, more distant, and more popular views of the falls. After crossing the Linville River on a footbridge from the visitor center, the level, road-width Linville Falls Trail leads through a scenic forest paralleling the river. A junction on the right at 0.4 mile is a Forest Service spur trail from NC 1238, a short distance away. (This trailhead makes a nice alternative starting point and positions you for a side trip to Wiseman's View.)

From the Linville Falls Trail, a side trail leads left to Upper Falls View, 0.5 mile from the visitor center, where the river funnels over its first big drop. Back on the main trail, the route rises through towering trees. White pine, oak, and birch trees complement this virgin hemlock forest. Here the trail starts a gradual rise to scrubbier vegetation associated with drier soils along the crags overlooking the gorge.

At 0.6 mile from the visitor center, another junction splits the trail at a rudimentary picnic/rain shelter. To the left the trail descends steep steps and reaches Chimney View at 0.7 mile, where hikers get an oft-photographed view of the entire falls. Back at the shelter, again head away from the visitor center as the trail climbs through dry, piney forest. Not far away on the right is Gorge View Overlook, a look down the gorge with an interpretive sign. The gorge appears again on the right, and on the left at about 1.0 mile is Erwins View, where the falls, gorge, and hikers on

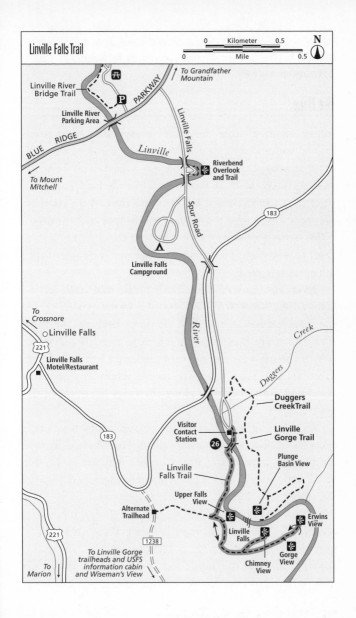

Linville Falls Trail

Kilometer
Mile

N

To Grandfather Mountain

Linville River Bridge Trail

PARKWAY

Linville River Parking Area

BLUE RIDGE

To Mount Mitchell

Linville

Linville Falls

Riverbend Overlook and Trail

183

Spur Road

Linville Falls Campground

To Crossnore

Linville Falls

Linville Falls Motel/Restaurant

221

183

River

Duggers *Creek*

Duggers Creek Trail

Visitor Contact Station

26

Linville Gorge Trail

Linville Falls Trail

Plunge Basin View

Upper Falls View

Alternate Trailhead

1238

To Linville Gorge trailheads and USFS information cabin and Wiseman's View

To Marion

221

Linville Falls

Chimney View

Gorge View

Erwins View

Chimney View are all in sight from the trail system's high point—about 3,360 feet. Retrace your steps from here for a 2.0-mile round-trip hike.

Whether or not you've started at the Forest Service's alternative trailhead on NC 1238, you'd do well to consider a side trip to Wiseman's View. It can be a dusty, 3.8-mile drive (one way), but the easy 0.2-mile trail to the rim of the gorge really gives you the flavor of this primitive cleft in the Blue Ridge.

Key Points

0.4 Forest Service spur trail from NC 1238.

0.5 Side trail left to Upper Falls View.

0.6 Junction left to Chimney View.

1.0 Erwins View.

27 Balsam Nature Trail (Milepost 355.3)

The Balsam Nature Trail is a self-guided interpretive trail that explores the spruce-fir forest and deforestation caused by acid rain.

Parkway milepost: Reached from Milepost 355.3
Distance: 0.8-mile loop
Difficulty: Easy

Elevation gain: Negligible
Maps: *USGS Mount Mitchell;* rudimentary state park map available at summit facilities

Finding the trailhead: Take NC 128, the state park access road from Parkway Milepost 355, and go all the way to the Mount Mitchell summit parking area. Walk past the concession stand/museum on the ascending paved trail toward the summit tower. Go left when the Old Mitchell Trail branches right and then take the next left for the Balsam Trail. (A right leads to the new, wheelchair accessible summit tower—and a not-to-be-missed view.)

The Hike

Mount Mitchell—the highest peak east of the Mississippi—is a crowning part of the Blue Ridge Parkway experience. The 1,700-acre Mount Mitchell State Park—North Carolina's first state park—clings to the highest peak of the Black Mountains and dominates the western skyline of North Carolina.

The story of how Mount Mitchell was named and measured involves considerable controversy. Although Connecticut native Elisha Mitchell is acknowledged as the first to measure the peak, Thomas Clingman, a North Carolinian, congressman, and senator, also claimed that he had been first. The debate went on for years until Mitchell returned to the peak and died in a slip from a waterfall. That swayed the public to Mitchell's side, and he was buried on his namesake summit in 1858. His grave still lies below the summit tower.

The white triangle–blazed Balsam Nature Trail explores Mitchell's mountain—the highest, most Northern climate in the South. The recently improved interpretive path has trailside exhibits that feature the ecosystem, climate, and plants and animals that live in this rarefied evergreen zone only found this far south at elevations above 5,500 feet. The pollution-induced dieback of the forest here is one topic tackled on the trail and in the mountain's recommended museum.

The dying trees have returned this forest to the early stages of succession one might expect to discover after a forest fire or clear-cutting. Early research had blamed the destruction of the mountain's evergreen zone on an infestation by the balsam woolly adelgid, a pest introduced into the United States around 1900. More recent studies suggest damage by acid rain—highly acidic precipitation that upsets the pH balance of the soil, freeing heavy metals that inhibit a tree's ability to ingest nutrients.

The latest research suggests that airborne pollution from upwind utilities and industries leads to startlingly high ozone levels on Southern summits. Such pollution, often contained in cloud caps as acidic as vinegar, burns the needles of firs, dramatically inhibiting the growth and survival of evergreens already fighting a severe climate. The result is the stark tree skeletons of Fraser fir and red spruce that stand tall and gray in ghostlike groves. The Balsam Nature Trail is an introduction to this ongoing ecological catastrophe.

In addition to the evergreen Fraser fir and red spruce, prevalent deciduous species at this elevation include mountain ash. Among other plants are many found in New England—hobblebush and mountain wood sorrel, or oxalis, a cloverlike ground covering associated with boreal forests. It blooms in late May and early June. The rhododendron blooms in late June. Yellow birch seen here also grows north to Minnesota and Quebec.

The first leg of the trail passes Camp Rock, an east-facing shelter ledge used by explorers as early as 1850. The damp seeps at similar outcrops along the trail are favored growing sites for the purple turtlehead, a snapdragon-like flower. There's a view north along the Black Mountain range. Mount Craig is the dominant, nearer summit just beyond the parking lot.

In addition to the yellow birch found on the trail, you might notice a grove of mountain paper birch, similar to the white-barked birches so often associated with New Hampshire and Vermont. The small heart-shaped leaves are the giveaway. If, as some scientists speculate, this grove is actually a separate species of birch, then only about 400 specimens exist, all within this state park.

The Balsam Nature Trail turns back left where the Old Mount Mitchell Trail goes straight to descend Commissary Ridge to Black Mountain Campground. This area is home to the most severe winter weather in North Carolina. In two days during March 1993, the mountain received a record 50 inches of snow. The trail passes a nearby stream that is likely the highest spring in eastern America. Its average temperature (when not frozen in winter) is 36 degrees

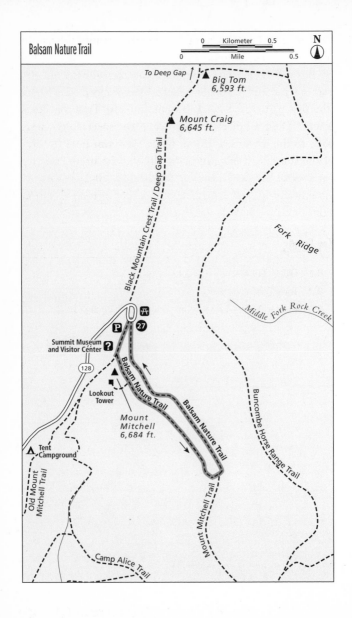

Balsam Nature Trail

0   Kilometer   0.5

0   Mile   0.5

N

To Deep Gap ↑

▲ Big Tom
6,593 ft.

▲ Mount Craig
6,645 ft.

Black Mountain Crest Trail / Deep Gap Trail

Fork Ridge

Middle Fork Rock Creek

P
🅰 27

Summit Museum
and Visitor Center ❓

128

▲
Lookout
Tower

Balsam Nature Trail

Balsam Nature Trail

Mount
Mitchell
6,684 ft.

Buncombe Horse Range Trail

Old Mount Mitchell Trail

▲ Tent
Campground

Mount Mitchell Trail

Camp Alice Trail

Fahrenheit. About 100 yards beyond the turnoff, the nature trail ends at the summit parking lot.

For a longer walk, leave from the opposite end of the parking lot and take the orange-blazed Deep Gap Trail (the first part of the Black Mountain Crest Trail that leads toward Deep Gap) to Mount Craig for spectacular views back to the tower on Mount Mitchell. From here the size of the summit development shrinks and the mountain you conquered by car gains in stature. It's a 2.0-mile moderate out-and-back day hike, with 535 feet of total elevation gain.

Key Points

0.1 Old Mount Mitchell Trail goes right.

0.2 Tower Trail goes right.

0.6 Balsam Nature Trail turns left from Mount Mitchell Trail.

28 Craggy Pinnacle Trail (Milepost 364.1)

Enjoy one of the Parkway's most inspiring 360-degree views from atop mysterious mountaintop meadows.

Parkway milepost: 364.1
Distance: 1.4 miles out and back
Difficulty: Moderate
Elevation gain: 252 feet

Maps: USGS Craggy Pinnacle; Parkway map available online at www.nps.gov/blri/planyourvisit/brochures.htm and in season at visitor center

Finding the trailhead: The Craggy Pinnacle Trail begins in the Craggy Dome Parking Area at Milepost 364, north of the visitor center and the Craggy Pinnacle Tunnel. A spur road leads to the parking area from the Parkway.

The Hike

How can names like Craggy Gardens, Craggy Dome, and Craggy Pinnacle not be magnets for hikers? Any Parkway motorist will likely agree that the Craggy Mountains' seemingly alpine, treeless environment of meadow- and heath-covered mountaintops represents some of the high road's most dramatic scenery. These Southern balds are among the most unique ecosystems in the Southern Appalachians.

The late-June bloom of rhododendron across the balds is one of the Southern Appalachians' premier natural events. Theories about the balds speculate that fires claimed the trees and made the soil unsuitable for immediate reforestation. Natural or even man-made fires, perhaps created by

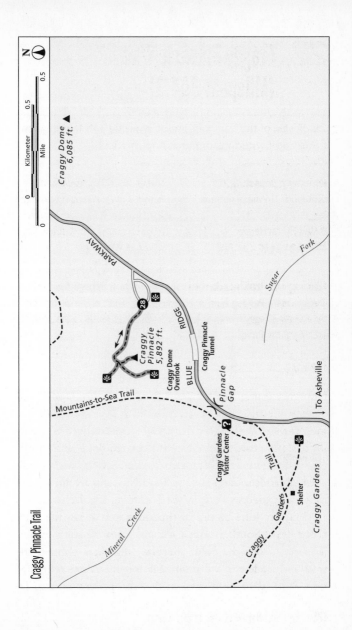

Craggy Pinnacle Trail

Native Americans to foster better conditions for game, could explain the existence of the meadows. Scientists are still uncertain how they originated.

Craggy Pinnacle affords the Craggies' premier view. The path climbs to 360-degree vistas at 5,892 feet. The Mount Mitchell range dominates the northern horizon. On a clear day, a veritable who's who of Southern Appalachian summits stand out in all directions.

From the start the path follows a gradually ascending rhododendron tunnel and then climbs up stone steps on the way to a trail junction at 0.3 mile where a FRAGILE HABITAT RARE PLANTS sign exhorts hikers to stay on the main trails and within the designated viewing spots. Three short trails diverge here. A hard right on an unsigned path past a resting bench wanders out a short ridge with views to the northwest.

Returning to the junction, follow the sign as it points to the middle trail, a lower overlook that looks down on the Craggy Gardens Visitor Center. Return again to the sign and go right to four stone-encircled viewpoints on top for stunning 360-degree views. Even on a wildly windy or overcast day, it's worth the short walk to soak up the otherworldly aura of the peak.

Key Points

0.3 View trail goes right.

0.7 Summit view.

29 Craggy Gardens Trail (Milepost 364.5)

Great views from spectacular mountaintop balds recommend two Craggy Gardens hikes of different lengths.

Parkway milepost: 364.5
Distance: 0.8 mile out and back from the visitor center; 1.2 miles out and back from the Craggy Gardens Picnic Area
Difficulty: Moderate

Elevation gain: About 145 feet
Maps: *USGS Craggy Pinnacle;* Parkway map available online at www.nps.gov/blri/planyourvisit/brochures.htm and in season at visitor center

Finding the trailhead: Craggy Gardens Visitor Center is on the Blue Ridge Parkway at Milepost 364.5, about 20 miles north of Asheville. The Craggy Gardens Trail begins on the south side of the visitor center.

A second trailhead is located west of the visitor center in the Craggy Gardens Picnic Area. To reach it, turn from the Parkway onto the unpaved Stoney Fork Road at Milepost 367.6. Take the next right into the picnic area and go to the end of the parking area.

The Hike

The Craggy Gardens Trail dips into the woods and the Mountains-to-Sea Trail goes right at 0.1 mile. Beyond, the path climbs gradually through a marvelously cylindrical rhododendron tunnel. This first section of the hike is a self-guiding nature trail, with resting benches and signs identifying plants.

The trail leaves the woods and levels out at grassy Craggy Flats at a rustic, recently restored picnic shelter built by the

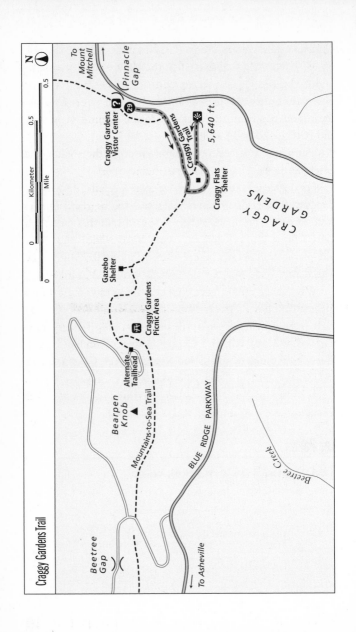

Craggy Gardens Trail

N

To Mount Mitchell

Pinnacle Gap

Kilometer

0.5   0.5

Mile

0   0.5

Craggy Gardens Vistor Center

29

Craggy Gardens Trail

5,640 ft.

Craggy Flats Shelter

CRAGGY GARDENS

Gazebo Shelter

Craggy Gardens Picnic Area

Alternate Trailhead

Bearpen Knob

Mountains-to-Sea Trail

BLUE RIDGE PARKWAY

Beetree Gap

To Asheville

Beetree Creek

Civilian Conservation Corps (CCC) in the 1930s. Side trails to the left just before and after the shelter lead across the wind-whipped grasses of the balds to a view from a stone observation platform at 5,640 feet. Retrace your steps and the round-trip from the Parkway to the summit viewpoint and back is about 0.8 mile.

The main trail continues right through the shelter and descends to the Craggy Gardens Picnic Area.

For a longer walk of just more than 1.0 mile, start in the Craggy Gardens Picnic Area. The trail climbs gradually and at about 0.3 mile passes a short leftward trail that leads to a view from a gazebo shelter. From this direction the rustic old picnic shelter at Craggy Flats is about 0.5 mile. The round-trip, including the summit, is about 1.2 miles.

Whichever route you choose, the grassy crest offers spectacular views. Vistas from the meadows near Craggy Flats picnic shelter look north to hikers atop Craggy Pinnacle (5,892 feet, left) and Craggy Dome (6,085 feet, right). The observation platform looks south over Craggy Knob (5,600 feet) and the Asheville Watershed's huge reservoir. Keep either of the two shelters in mind if the weather threatens (as it can quickly at this elevation).

Key Points

0.3   Left turn at Craggy Flats picnic shelter.

The Southern Appalachians

Mileposts 384.7 (US 74 at Asheville) to 469.1 (US 441 at Great Smoky Mountains NP)

Literally the loftiest part of the Parkway, the section from US 74 in Asheville (Milepost 384.7) to Great Smoky Mountains National Park (Milepost 469.1) has a feel all its own. It soars across the highest landmasses traversed by the high road. Add to that the sheer acreage of surrounding national forest lands, and you have a high and away-from-it-all experience that's second to none.

This is where the Blue Ridge meets the jumble of mountain ranges that make up the vast heart of the Southern Appalachians. On your way to Cherokee, North Carolina, and a memorable meeting with the massive wall of the Great Smokies, the mountaintop route surveys a mountain empire unmatched in eastern America. But off-Parkway options are nearby and noteworthy.

Asheville must lead that list—indeed, more Parkway visitors enter and exit the Parkway in Asheville than at any other place. Try the city's Urban Trail for an introduction to its vibrant downtown culture.

The biggest attraction is Biltmore House and Gardens, George W. Vanderbilt's 250-room summer place that is the United States' largest home. Its breathtaking gardens, interiors, and artwork are simply a must-see part of a Parkway experience. There's bike and horseback riding and kayaking, and the new Inn on Biltmore Estate is a perfect platform for estate-raised foods and wines.

Festivals are an Asheville forte, with crafts and music as a focus. July's Belle Chere is the state's largest street fest. And August boasts the Mountain Dance and Folk Festival, the nation's oldest event focused on mountain music.

The literary heritage of the Appalachians and the increasing popularity of modern fiction about the mountains are most apparent here. Visit Thomas Wolfe's boyhood home before you, yourself, go home again. Both Wolfe and O. Henry (William Sydney Porter) are buried in Asheville's Riverside Cemetery. You can make the short side trip to Carl Sandburg's home, Connemara, at nearby Hendersonville. Later, from the Parkway gaze at Cold Mountain, setting of the National Book Award–winning best seller.

Parkway travelers can literally check into local literary heritage at the Grove Park Inn, among the most quintessential Appalachian hotels. The preserved historic heart of the inn, with its massive fireplace, has a room that was frequently occupied by F. Scott Fitzgerald. It's a favorite with readers. The hotel is renowned for top-notch facilities, including a new and nationally significant spa.

Once you're out of the city, this southernmost section of the Parkway has classic mountain towns that are at their liveliest during summer. Drop in (literally, from the Parkway) on Highlands, Cashiers, Rosman, and Brevard (with its internationally known summer music festival, held June to August).

Indeed, this is one of the best places to hop off the Parkway and take side loops.

After driving this National Park Service route, the Forest Heritage Scenic Byway is a perfect way to sample the best of the national forests flanking the road. One of the United States' most popular scenic byways, this 79-mile national forest circuit crosses the Parkway on both sides of Shining Rock Wilderness and follows US 276, NC 215, and US 64 in the vicinity of Brevard. The trip includes the "Cradle of Forestry" facility, the nation's earliest forestry school.

This is the "Land of Waterfalls." Looking Glass Falls is one of the roadside attractions of the Forest Heritage Byway, as is the national forest's natural water slide, Sliding Rock. Many national forest campgrounds and picnic areas line the route.

Other tours from town include Handmade in America's seven craft heritage routes. From Asheville's eateries, with a focus on locally grown seasonal produce, to the newly opened Grove Arcade Market downtown and on to out-of-the-way craft shops and galleries, these mountains are a hotbed of tradition.

This is the city where the Southern Highland Handicraft Guild was born, and the Parkway's Folk Art Center, just north of the city, is a showcase for the work of its members. Many, many other galleries are all over town, some in unique shopping settings like Biltmore Village, a multiblock neighborhood of historic homes converted to distinctive shops. Here also is the Parkway Visitor Center (Milepost 384). The brand new, primary visitor center for the road is just in time for the Parkway's seventy-fifth anniversary.

The green building has a meadow-covered roof and exhibits on the Parkway's vistas, history, geology, and culture. An interactive wall map covers the entire journey. And there's a large bookstore, theater, and restrooms.

Save time for Cherokee. The tribe's stirring culture and history come alive at Unto These Hills, an outdoor drama that tells the Trail of Tears saga (early June to late August). The Museum of the Cherokee Indian has top-notch interactive exhibits. Oconaluftee Indian Village re-creates a Cherokee town. Craft and fine artworks by members of the oldest Native American art organization are available at the Qualla Arts and Crafts Mutual, Inc.

Between the French Broad and Nantahala Rivers, and many other watercourses, this is the best part of the Parkway for canoeing, kayaking, or whitewater rafting.

The Asheville area is full of film locations. Not far east of town is scenic Lake Lure (*Dirty Dancing*) and Chimney Rock, the latter a trail-laced natural area where the most memorable scenes from *The Last of the Mohicans* were filmed. Anywhere you go in Asheville—and especially as you take the Parkway in and out—you'll marvel at the city's cinematic setting.

30 Buck Spring Trail (Mileposts 407.7–411.8)

A largely graded trail makes a pleasant walk from the Pisgah Inn to the site of George Vanderbilt's Buck Spring Hunting Lodge.

Parkway mileposts: 407.7, 408.6, and 411.8
Distance: 1.6 miles to 3.1 miles out and back
Difficulty: Easy to moderate
Elevation gain: About 480 feet from Pisgah Inn to hunting lodge site and back

Maps: *USGS Dunsmore Mountain and Cruso;* Parkway Mount Pisgah map available online at www.nps.gov/blri/planyourvisit/brochures.htm and in season at lodge, campground, and other facilities

Finding the trailhead: On the south end (Milepost 408.6), park in the lot at the Pisgah Inn and start beside the trail map sign at the parking area's north end. Alternatively, on the north end, park at Buck Spring Gap Overlook (Milepost 407.7). You can also walk between the lodge office and the restaurant, descend the stone steps, and follow the grassy path right to US 276. To start there, at the bottom of the trail, most of which is on USDA Forest Service property, drive to Milepost 411.8 and then go south on US 276 for 2 miles; park on the left.

The Hike

This pleasant path is a perfect place for an aimless amble, particularly for lodge or campground guests.

The Buck Spring Trail is predominately used as an untaxing walk to the site of Vanderbilt's hunting lodge for people starting from the Pisgah Inn, on the Parkway's section of the trail. The trail leaves the area of the inn at the map sign, passes a junction on the right with the Thompson Creek Trail and then lodge employee housing on the left, gains a ridge at 0.3 mile, and at 0.6 mile passes the Pilot Rock Trail. That trail goes a bit more than 2.0 miles to Yellow Gap Road. (In that direction, the path reaches the summit of Little Bald Mountain 0.2 mile from the Buck Spring Trail—a nice side trip or turnaround point for a round-trip of 1.6 miles.)

Just 0.1 mile beyond that junction, the Laurel Mountain Trail also goes right, this time to Yellow Gap Road in 7.0 miles. Keeping to the Buck Spring Trail, you reach the lodge site at 1.0 mile (just 0.1 mile beyond is Buck Spring Gap Overlook). Interpretive signs describe the history of buildings that were removed in 1963. That's a 1.0-mile walk for a 2.0-mile round-trip (2.4 miles if you take in Little Bald Mountain's summit). Much of both of these routes is part of the Mountains-to-Sea Trail.

Another option is to return to your car at the lodge via the Mount Pisgah Trail and picnic area connector. To do that, go to the other end of Buck Spring Gap Overlook, the upper trailhead for the Shut-In Trail. Heading into the woods, hike to the next parking lot, the start of the Mount Pisgah Trail, at about 1.3 miles. Switch to the Mount Pisgah Trail and immediately turn left onto the picnic area connector. Cross the parking lot at the picnic area at about 1.9 miles and continue toward the campground. Pass the side trail to a no-name parking area. As the campsites appear off to the right, go left on the trail to the Parkway at about 3.0

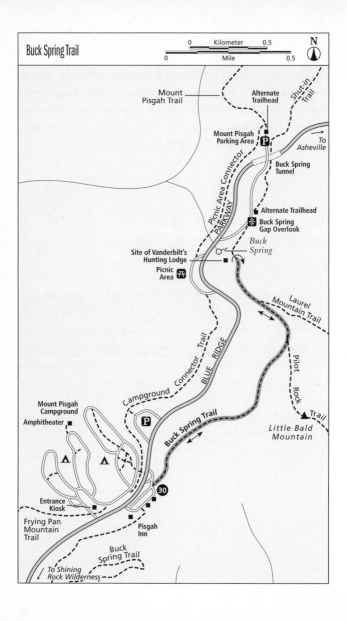

Buck Spring Trail

Kilometer
0   0.5

Mile
0   0.5

N

Mount Pisgah Trail

Alternate Trailhead

Shut-in Trail

Mount Pisgah Parking Area

To Asheville

Picnic Area Connector

PARKWAY

Buck Spring Tunnel

Alternate Trailhead

Buck Spring Gap Overlook

Site of Vanderbilt's Hunting Lodge

Buck Spring

Picnic Area

Laurel Mountain Trail

Campground Connector Trail

BLUE RIDGE

Pilot Rock Trail

Buck Spring Trail

Little Bald Mountain

Mount Pisgah Campground

Amphitheater

Buck Spring Trail

Entrance Kiosk

Frying Pan Mountain Trail

Pisgah Inn

30

Buck Spring Trail

To Shining Rock Wilderness

miles. Cross the road past the gas station to the parking area for about a 3.1-mile hike.

The easiest route to the old lodge location is to start at the north end of the trail at the Buck Spring Gap Overlook. From there the lodge site is 0.1 mile. Along the way, informal paths lead left to the edge of the ridge—surely viewpoints in Vanderbilt's time.

Key Points

0.6 Pass Pilot Rock Trail.

0.7 Laurel Mountain Trail goes right.

1.0 Arrive at site of Buck Spring Hunting Lodge.

For a not-so-easy hike option—due to its length of 12 miles—you might want to tackle the lengthy Forest Service portion of the Buck Spring Trail. It leaves US 276, passes junctions left and right respectively with the Mountains-to-Sea Trail and the MST alternate at 1.0 mile and 1.2, and climbs gradually through very scenic vegetation with many small stream crossings. The path switchbacks more steeply to an old road grade and then becomes grassy as it reaches the front of the Pisgah Inn at about 6.0 miles. From that lowest trailhead, the inn could be a great hike to lunch at the restaurant for a long but doable 12.0-mile round-trip.

31 Graveyard Fields Trails and Black Balsam Knob (Mileposts 418.8 and 420.2)

A loop hike reaches a spectacular waterfall and explores a high, alpinelike valley, while an out–and–back route bags an awesome bald summit.

Parkway mileposts: 418.8 and 420.2
Distance: 2.0-mile loop with a 1.4-mile option; 0.8 mile out and back to Black Balsam Knob
Difficulty: Easy to moderately challenging (with easy backpacking for beginners)

Elevation gain: 300 feet for the 2.0-mile loop (700 feet for the 3.4-mile loop); 300 feet for Balsam Knob
Maps: USGS Shining Rock; Pisgah National Forest's Shining Rock–Middle Prong Wilderness map covers area best

Finding the trailhead: The trail begins at Graveyard Fields Overlook, Milepost 418.8 on the Blue Ridge Parkway, 30 miles south of US 25 in Asheville. The trail is about 7 miles south of the US 276 junction and about 4.5 miles north of the NC 215 junction.

The Hikes

As you drive south out of Asheville and climb past Mount Pisgah, the Shining Rock Wilderness can't help but catch your attention. The horizon peels back on an almost Western scale, and meadow-covered mountaintops march off to meet summits cloaked in evergreens and accented by milk-white crags of quartz—the area's namesake "shining rocks." The Graveyard Fields Trail explores a scenic valley just below these summits.

Hikes on the well-maintained but heavily traveled Graveyard Fields Loop can range from a short out-and-back hike to a full-length streamside loop, with or without scenic waterfalls. Though this lofty area—the trailhead is at 5,100 feet and the high point 5,400 feet—never gets very warm, the pool below Lower or Second Falls is a great summer spot to cool off.

One caution: Probably the most daunting part of the entire hike is the steep descent from the Blue Ridge Parkway to the stream valley. It's short, only a few tenths of a mile, but it is steep on the way back up if you return the same way. (The return described here climbs much more gradually.) Otherwise the Graveyard Fields Loop is a relatively easy way to explore a lofty area near the Shining Rock Wilderness, one of the state's most scenic areas.

The logged open fields here were named following a devastating fire in 1925. The thousands of stumps remaining reminded some people of grave markers. The entire watershed was consumed by wildfires in the 1920s and again in the 1940s; the little valley burned again in the late 1990s. The earliest massive fires gave the Shining Rock area its above–tree line appearance; the results of the 25,000- and 50,000-acre conflagrations can still be seen in the largely treeless landscape. Few places in North Carolina afford better views.

This gentle stream valley makes the perfect place for a day hike, picnic, or backpacking trip, especially for beginners or those who want scenic camping without arduous walking. The area is very popular in summer and fall, though, so campers in this fragile area should observe scrupulous camping practices. Although accessible campsites

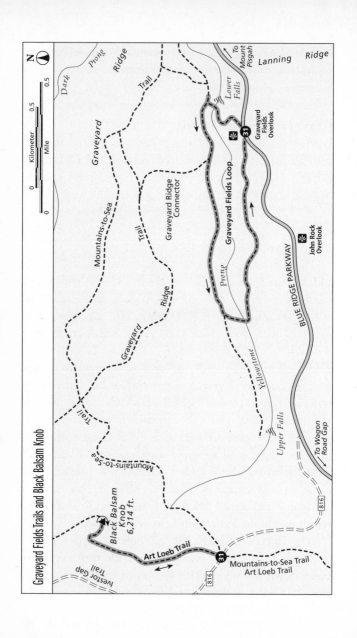

Graveyard Fields Trails and Black Balsam Knob

N

Kilometer
0   0.5

Mile
0   0.5

Dark Prong Ridge

Lanning Ridge

To Mount Pisgah

Lower Falls

Graveyard Fields Overlook

31

Graveyard Ridge Trail

Graveyard Ridge Connector

Graveyard Fields Loop

Mountains-to-Sea Trail

Prong

John Rock Overlook

BLUE RIDGE PARKWAY

Yellowstone

Mountains-to-Sea Trail

Upper Falls

To Wagon Road Gap

816

Black Balsam Knob
6,214 ft.

Art Loeb Trail

Nestor Gap Trail

816

31

Mountains-to-Sea Trail
Art Loeb Trail

may be filled during the busy seasons, it is easy to find out-of-the-way sites for zero-impact camping. Best advice for campers—go during the week.

Graveyard Fields Loop

Leaving the right side of the Parkway overlook, the trail descends the steep paved path to wood steps and a boardwalk bridge across Yellowstone Prong. Go right at the junction beyond, signed to LOWER FALLS, and cross a small bridge. Descend another elaborate sloping wooden boardwalk with steps to the base of the cataract with a deep pool beneath it (called Second Falls on the topo map).

Retrace your steps to the junction, at about 0.5 mile, and continue past the split-rail fence with the GRAVEYARD FIELDS/UPPER FALLS sign. This is a place of plentiful side trails, so watch closely as you emerge into the open meadows on a worn path along more fence. Views reach up to the balds above, along the skyline of the Art Loeb Trail and Shining Rock Wilderness. All around, evergreens mingle with deciduous trees and blueberry bushes. Beyond a boardwalk, bear right. (A side trail left dead-ends at a campsite by the stream, where you could mistake fishing trails for the path upriver.) Soon meet the Graveyard Ridge Connector branching right at an unsigned junction. Stay left and you'll cross a short boardwalk over a drainage that confirms your choice. Good campsites become visible as you arrive at the loop's final signed junction, at the 1.0-mile mark. The return part of the loop heads left over the bridge.

The right-hand trail goes 0.7 mile to Upper Falls, a much less visited, more precipitous cascade with impressive views down the valley. This section of trail, a side trip of about 1.4 miles, is steeper and rockier than the rest of the route and would up the elevation gain of the hike to a not-insignificant 700 feet. If you take this option, retrace your steps downstream from Upper Falls and take a right turn across Yellowstone Prong at about 2.7 miles.

The return route gradually ascends through boggy areas with a high-altitude feel. You'll cross bog logs and a sloping boardwalk on the way and be back at the parking lot in about 0.5 mile (this time climbing a short flight of wood steps to the left side of the overlook). Including Upper Falls, the entire hike is about 3.4 miles and moderately challenging. Without the Upper Falls, the 2.0-mile loop is rated moderately easy.

Key Points

0.5   Arrive back at bridge after side trip to lower waterfall.

1.0   Return leg of loop goes left; side trail to Upper Falls goes right.

2.0   Arrive back at parking area (about 3.4 miles with side trail to Upper Falls).

Black Balsam Knob

If you can't resist the lure of the summits, take the Parkway south to Milepost 420.2 and go right on FSR 816. Park below Black Balsam Knob on the right 0.8 mile from the Parkway. Take the Art Loeb Trail and quickly ascend in 0.4 mile to the open vistas and waving grasses of Black Balsam Knob (6,214 feet). This view is among the best along the Parkway. North, the Mount Mitchell range bulks beyond Asheville, with the High Country resort area and Grandfather Mountain beyond that. The Smokies rise dramatically to the west. This is a short, steeper hike (take your time!) to a 360-degree panorama worthy of bringing your binoculars and a camera.

32 Richland Balsam Self-Guiding Trail (Milepost 431.0)

Numbered posts keyed to an interpretive brochure describe the changing composition of a lofty spruce-fir forest at 6,410 feet—the highest elevation reached by a Parkway trail.

Parkway milepost: 431.0
Distance: 1.4-mile loop
Difficulty: Moderate

Elevation gain: 390 feet
Maps: *USGS Sam Knob;* no Parkway map

Finding the trailhead: The trail starts at the Haywood-Jackson Overlook (named for the boundary of the two counties), 9.2 miles south of NC 215.

The Hike

Here's an oddity—a rooty trail a lot like the backcountry tracks that wind everywhere in western North Carolina's national forests. The Richland Balsam Trail is the perfect counterpoint to the Parkway's generally groomed paths. It's a reminder that nature's "beauty" can be untidy and unkempt—and more real in its roughness. And it's also the Parkway's best path to experience the aromatic lushness of the dripping, cloud-dampened spruce-fir forest.

Before you start your hike, enjoy the fine view of the Shining Rock Wilderness on the overlook's skyline. Prominent peaks run from Cold Mountain on the left to the gentle pyramid of Mount Pisgah, the white-quartz summit of Shining Rock, and on to Devil's Courthouse on the far right.

Just up the paved first 100 yards of the trail is a brochure box with laminated trail guides to borrow for your hike. The theme here, as it is at Mount Mitchell State Park's Balsam Nature Trail, is a Fraser fir forest in decline. The brochure's twenty-plus interpretive stops explore the topic.

Go right after the pavement ends at the first two of many benches, these in a tiny clearing where the loop splits. The trail passes an odd mileage sign (3,100 FEET TO THE SUMMIT) and then winds around through dense summer growths of sedge grasses and briers.

The trail passes rich evergreen zone vegetation and a sign reading 1,600 FEET TO SUMMIT. It rises over a series of small peaks to a bench at 0.6 mile, where the summit sign reads 6,410 feet. The path drops off the back of the peak, descending flights of stone steps amid evergreens and grasses. The evergreen needle–carpeted trail levels off and glides through a very scenic fir forest full of ferns.

A faint side trail goes right to the top of the road-cut with views of the Richland Balsam Overlook, the next view south on the Parkway (highest point on the motor road). You'll pass another few benches at 1.2 miles, the second with the trail's best view—a look along the Parkway to Cowee Mountain Overlook, the next overlook heading north. The trail passes through more spruce forest and ferns to the loop junction and a right back to the parking area at about 1.4 miles.

Even on a warm dry day, the summit shade is cool, which explains the seemingly drunken bumblebees fighting to do their summer duty amid the gusty chill. It's that evergreen forest feeling that recommends this trail. If that feeling, and not the summit is your goal, just go left when the loop starts for a short, easy, and atmospheric out-and-back walk to the last few benches. (Oh . . . don't forget to return your brochure to the box.)

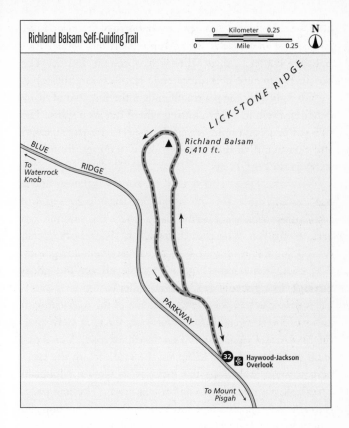

Key Points

- **0.2** Loop branches; go right.
- **0.6** Summit bench.
- **1.2** Bench with good view.
- **1.3** Loop returns.
- **1.4** Parking lot.

33 Waterrock Knob Trail (Milepost 451.2)

This steep paved path climbs from one of the Parkway's small visitor centers to a designated must-see viewpoint. The hike continues on a rougher path to the wilder summit of Waterrock Knob (6,292 feet).

Parkway milepost: 451.2
Distance: 1.2 miles out and back

Difficulty: Moderate to more challenging
Maps: *USGS Sylva North;* no Parkway map

Finding the trailhead: Park in the Waterrock Knob Visitor Center parking lot and ascend the paved path.

The Hike

Waterrock Knob is one of the key viewpoints that recommend the high-altitude southernmost section of the Blue Ridge Parkway. Luckily there are two sides to this steep and more challenging trail that make it a suitable walk for less-than-serious hikers.

The trail soars out of the parking area as a steep and paved path. Take your time; a bench appears just where the grade slackens to nearly level. Not far beyond on the left, notice the huge fan-shaped root system of a wind-downed spruce. The solid rock barely below the soil surface explains the shape of the root system and illustrates the challenge faced by these high-altitude evergreens.

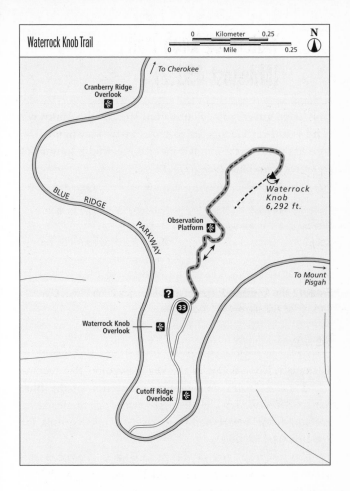

Kilometer

0   0.25

Mile

0   0.25

N

↑ To Cherokee

Cranberry Ridge
Overlook

BLUE RIDGE PARKWAY

Waterrock
Knob
6,292 ft.

Observation
Platform

To Mount
Pisgah

?

33

Waterrock Knob
Overlook

Cutoff Ridge
Overlook

The trail ascends past another bench before switchback-
ing up two flights of stone steps to a rock wall–encircled
observation point. The mountains ripple away; below, the
Parkway arcs across a mountainside. This is the place to head
back if you're unsure of foot or tired.

Above the viewpoint, the trail rises over steps, becomes rocky then gravel covered, and levels out as it leaves the evergreens and enters an open meadow of filamentous ferns where northern white hellebore still grows in July. There's a bench in this clearing. Farther on, the trail gets rougher, eroded in some spots, and ascends steeply, at times over crags and one flight of steep stone steps. The trail winds around the back of the peak on switchbacks with stone steps to a nice view into Maggie Valley. The trail climbs again, and after a last flight of steps reaches an evergreen-bordered bench on the largely open top of Waterrock Knob at 6,292 feet.

More than 80 percent of mature firs on this part of the Parkway have died from the balsam woolly adelgid, and the destruction is evident here and in many places on the way up. If you walk the informal path over the crest, you can descend through the lush meadow greenery (annual rainfall exceeds 60 inches on the summit) and actually peer down on the parking lot.

Key Points

0.1 First bench.

0.2 Developed viewpoint.

0.6 Summit bench.

About the Author

Randy Johnson is a widely published authority on the Appalachian outdoors and has lived near the Parkway most of his life. He's the author of the bestselling guidebooks *Hiking North Carolina* and *Hiking the Blue Ridge Parkway* (both FalconGuides), among others. Articles and photos by this award-winning photojournalist have for decades brought the Appalachians to readers of national magazines, newspapers, and major outdoor Web sites. As editor of the country's most award-winning airline magazine, he often focused on accessible adventure.

A trail designer and builder, Randy was the founding wilderness manager at Grandfather Mountain and helped ensure the preservation of this significant North Carolina summit as a United Nations–designated biosphere reserve and now a state park. He was a trail design consultant for the Parkway's Tanawha Trail and worked to mesh the then private and Park Service trails into the system in place today. Randy was instrumental in making the Tanawha Trail part of the Mountains-to-Sea Trail, and as co-chairman of the Central Blue Ridge Task Force, he helped design and construct a portion of that statewide path. He's a longtime resident of the North Carolina mountains and lives in Banner Elk.

Visit www.randyjohnsonbooks.com to check out his television and radio appearances, videos, and publications, to send him an e-mail, and to see much more.